The Royal Hunt of the Sun

A Play Concerning the Conquest of Peru

Peter Shaffer

D1494565

**PLEASE DO
NOT WRITE
IN THIS BOOK**

Samuel French - London
New York - Toronto - Hollywood

Learning
Resource Centre   822 SHA
Stockton
Riverside College

© 1964 BY PETER SHAFFER

Rights of Performance by Amateurs are controlled by Samuel French Ltd, 52 Fitzroy Street, London W1T 5JR, and they, or their authorized agents, issue licences to amateurs on payment of a fee. **It is an infringement of the Copyright to give any performance or public reading of the play before the fee has been paid and the licence issued.**

The Royalty Fee indicated below is subject to contract and subject to variation at the sole discretion of Samuel French Ltd.

Basic fee for each and every
performance by amateurs   Code M
in the British Isles

The Professional Repertory Rights in this play are controlled by Samuel French Ltd. Professional Rights, other than Repertory, are controlled by Macnaughton Lord 2000 Ltd, 19 Margravine Gardens, London, W6 8RL

The publication of this play does not imply that it is necessarily available for performance by amateurs or professionals, either in the British Isles or Overseas. Amateurs and professionals considering a production are strongly advised in their own interests to apply to the appropriate agents for written consent before starting rehearsals or booking a theatre or hall.

ISBN 0 573 01388 8
ISBN 978 0573 013881

Please see page iv for further copyright information

The full score for Marc Wilkinson's music can be obtained from London Management Ltd, 14 Floral Street, London, WC2E 9DH

THE CHARACTERS

The Spaniards

The officers:
FRANCISCO PIZARRO, Commander of the Expedition
HERNANDO DE SOTO, Second-in-Command
MIGUEL ESTETE, Royal Veedor, or Overseer
DE CANDIA, Commander of Artillery
DIEGO DE TRUJILLO, Master of Horse

The Men:
MARTIN RUIZ
YOUNG MARTIN, Pizarro's Page: Old Martin as a boy
SALINAS, Blacksmith
RODAS, Tailor
VASCA
DOMINGO
JUAN CHAVEZ

The Priests:
FRAY VINCENTE DE VALVERDE, Chaplain to the Expedition
   (Dominican)
FRAY MARCOS DE NIZZA, Franciscan Friar

The Indians

ATAHUALLPA, Sovereign Inca of Peru
VILLAC UMU, High Priest of Peru
CHALLCUCHIMA, An Inca General
A CHIEFTAIN
A HEADSMAN OF A THOUSAND FAMILIES
FELIPILLO, An Indian boy, employed by Pizarro as Interpreter
MANCO, A Chasqui, or Messenger
INTI COUSSI, Stepsister of Atahuallpa ⎫ non-speaking parts
OELLO, A wife of Atahuallpa ⎭
        Spanish Soldiers and Peruvian Indians

PLACE—Apart from two early scenes in Spain and Panama, the play is set in the Upper Province of the Inca Empire; what is now South Ecuador and North-Western Peru. The whole of Act II takes place in the town of Cajamarca.

TIME: June 1529–August 1533

ACT ONE—THE HUNT   ACT TWO—THE KILL

COPYRIGHT INFORMATION

(See also page ii)

This play is fully protected under the Copyright Laws of the British Common-wealth of Nations, the United States of America and all countries of the Berne and Universal Copyright Conventions.

All rights including Stage, Motion Picture, Radio, Television, Public Reading, and Translation into Foreign Languages, are strictly reserved.

No part of this publication may lawfully be reproduced in ANY form or by any means — photocopying, typescript, recording (including video-recording), manuscript, electronic, mechanical, or otherwise—or be transmitted or stored in a retrieval system, without prior permission.

Licences for amateur performances are issued subject to the understanding that it shall be made clear in all advertising matter that the audience will witness an amateur performance; that the names of the authors of the plays shall be included on all programmes; and that the integrity of the authors' work will be preserved.

The Royalty Fee is subject to contract and subject to variation at the sole discretion of Samuel French Ltd.

In Theatres or Halls seating Four Hundred or more the fee will be subject to negotiation.

In Territories Overseas the fee quoted above may not apply. A fee will be quoted on application to our local authorized agent, or if there is no such agent, on application to Samuel French Ltd, London.

VIDEO-RECORDING OF AMATEUR PRODUCTIONS

Please note that the copyright laws governing video-recording are extremely complex and that it should not be assumed that any play may be video-recorded for whatever purpose without first obtaining the permission of the appropriate agents. The fact that a play is published by Samuel French Ltd does not indicate that video rights are available or that Samuel French Ltd controls such rights.

AUTHOR'S NOTES

THE TEXT

Each Act contains twelve sections, marked by Roman numerals. These are solely for reference, and do not indicate pauses or breaks of any kind. The action is continuous.

THE SET

Essentially, all that is required for a production of *The Royal Hunt of the Sun* is a bare stage and an upper level. However, the setting by Michael Annals was so superb, and so brilliantly succeeded in solving the visual problems of the play, that I wish to recall it here in print.

Basically this design consisted of a huge aluminium ring, twelve feet in diameter, hung in the centre of a plain wooden back-wall. Around its circumference were hinged twelve petals. When closed, these interlocked to form a great medallion on which was incised the emblem of the *Conquistadores*; when opened, they formed the rays of a giant golden sun, emblem of the Incas. Each petal had an inlay of gold magnetized to it: when these inlays were pulled out (in Act II, Scene vi) the great black frame remaining symbolized magnificently the desecration of Peru. The centre of this sun formed an acting area above the stage, which was used in Act I to show Atahuallpa in majesty, and in Act II served for his prison and subsequently for the treasure chamber.

This simple but amazing set was for me totally satisfying on all levels: scenically, aesthetically, and symbolically.

THE MUSIC

The musical experts at the end of the book represent the three most easily detached pieces from the remarkable score composed for the play by Marc Wilkinson. This extraordinary music I believe to be an integral part of any production of *The Royal Hunt of the Sun*. It embraces bird cries; plainchant; a fantasia for organ; freezing sounds for the Mime of the Great Ascent, and frightening ones for the Mime of the Great Massacre. To me its most memorable items are the exquisitely doleful lament which opens Act II, and, most amazing of all, the final Chant of Resurrection, to be whined and whispered, howled and hooted, over Atahuallpa's body in the darkness, before the last sunrise of the Inca Empire.

THE PRODUCTION

There are, no doubt, as many ways of producing this play, as there are of setting it. My hope was always to realize on stage a kind of 'total' theatre, involving not only words but rites, mimes, masks and magics. The text cries for illustration. It is a director's piece, a pantomimist's piece, a musician's piece, a designer's piece, and of course an actor's piece, almost as much as it is an author's. In this edition, as with the set, I have included as many details of the Chichester production as possible, partly because I was deeply involved in its creation, but mainly as a tribute to the superb achievement of John Dexter.

GENERAL NOTE ON THE PLAYING OF THE ROYAL HUNT OF THE SUN

The style in which the Spaniards are played should vary extremely and observably from that in which the Incas are played.

I think it will help if the Incas are played less naturalistically—certainly in a less Western way—than the Spaniards. They should be masked (half masks in gold) to suggest the relentless uniformity imposed on them by their social structure, with its absolute discouragement of individual feature. All hair styles should be the same: deep black, in formal cut, straight and 'South American Indian', and ponchos of the same colour or colours—suggesting, where possible, the use of vegetable dyes.

The walk, posture and speech of the Incas should be highly stylized: formalized gestures for the peasants and hieretic gestures for the court should be used throughout—together with cries, bird calls, chanting, wailing and the stylized speech patterns. Atahuallpa himself should be a creature of extreme unfamiliarity and unexpectedness to the audience. A possible image which suggests itself to me is the Firebird: elegant, remote, dazzling, and—like many god figures—bi-sexual (not effeminate, but giving the effect in the literal sense, of self-sufficiency). It is important to avoid at all times, in playing him or his subjects, even the faintest suggestion of mock-Oriental, theatrical-bizarre, or—even worse—the noble 'Me Great Chief' effect of American Western films. Actors should try to suggest the remote, very foreign and now defunct world of pre-Columbian America.

As for the staging, austerity and non-literalness should be the key-notes. Avoid realism, and conjure effects (with the help of lighting of course) of jungles and mountains; and the immense over-organized ritual of Inca life from placing, gesture and acting choices. The thought here is, say, Kabuki theatre filtered through English consciousness: everything, the marching, the fighting, the collection of the treasure and the treasure itself, and in particular the final lament in immense funeral masks, punctuated by long silences—should be informed with a powerful sense of ritual and imaginative suggestion.

Wherever possible the music of Marc Wilkinson for this play should be used. I regard it as an integral part of the play, and it will perfectly set the tone of the whole performance.

P.S.

ACT I

THE HUNT

Scene i

SCENE—*A bare stage. On the back wall, which is of wood, hangs a huge metal medallion, quartered by four black crucifixes sharpened to resemble swords.*

When the LIGHTS *come up, the stage is empty.* OLD MARTIN, *a grizzled man in his middle fifties, enters. He wears the black costume of a Spanish hidalgo in the mid-sixteenth century.*

Light
cue 1

OLD MARTIN. Save you all. My name is Martin. I'm a soldier of Spain and that's it. Most of my life I've spent fighting for land, treasure and the cross. I'm worth millions. Soon I'll be dead and they'll bury me out here in Peru, the land I helped ruin as a boy. This story is about ruin. Ruin and gold. More gold than any of you will ever see, even if you work in a counting house. I'm going to tell you how one hundred and sixty-seven men conquered an empire of twenty-four million. And then things that no one has ever told: things to make you groan and cry out I'm lying. And perhaps I am. The air of Peru is cold and sour like a vault, and wits turn easier here even than in Europe. But grant me this: I saw him closer than anyone, and had cause only to love him. He was my altar, my bright image of salvation. Francisco Pizarro! Time was when I'd have died for him, or for any worship.

(YOUNG MARTIN *enters, duelling an invisible opponent with a stick. He is Old Martin as an impetuous boy of fifteen*)

If you could only imagine what it was like for me at the beginning, to be allowed to serve him. But boys don't dream like that any more —service! Conquest! Riding down Indians in the name of Spain. The inside of my head was one vast plain for feats of daring. I used to lie up in the hayloft for hours reading my Bible—Don Cristobal on the rules of Chivalry. And then he came and made them real. And the only wish of my life is that I had never met him.

Light
cue 2

FRANCISCO PIZARRO *enters. He is a man in late middle age: tough, commanding, harsh, wasted, secret. The gestures are blunt and often violent: the expression intense and energetic, capable of fury and cruelty, but also of sudden melancholy and sardonic humour. At the moment he appears more neatly than he is ever to do again: hair and beard are trimmed, and his clothes quite grand, as if he is trying to make a fine impression. He is accompanied by his Second-in-Command,* HERNANDO DE SOTO, *and the Dominican* FRAY VINCENTE DE VALVERDE. DE SOTO *is an impressive figure in his forties: his whole air breathes an unquestioning loyalty—to his profession, his faith, and to accepted values. He is an admirable soldier and a staunch friend.* VALVERDE, *on the other hand, is a peasant priest whose zeal is not greatly tempered by intelligence, nor sweetened by an anxiety to please)*

PIZARRO. I was suckled by a sow. My house is the oldest in Spain —the pigsty.

OLD MARTIN. He'd made two expeditions to the New World already. Now, at over sixty years old, he was back in Spain, making one last try. He'd shown the King enough gold to get sole right of discovery in Peru, and the title of Viceroy over anything he conquered. In return he was to fit out an army at his own expense. He started recruiting in his own birthplace, Trujillo.

(*Several* VILLAGERS *enter, among them* SALINAS, *a blacksmith,* RODAS, *a tailor,* VASCA, DOMINGO *and the* CHAVEZ *brothers.*

PIZARRO *addresses* DIEGO, *a young man of twenty-five)*

PIZARRO. What's your name?
DIEGO. Diego, sir.
PIZARRO. What do you know best?
DIEGO. Horses, I suppose, if I was to name anything.
PIZARRO. And how would you feel to be Master of Horse, Diego?
DIEGO (*eagerly*) Sir!
PIZARRO. Who's smith here?
SALINAS. I am.
PIZARRO. Are you with us?
SALINAS. I'm not against you.
PIZARRO. What's your friend?
RODAS. Tailor, if it is your business.
PIZARRO. Well, soldiers never stop mending and patching. They'll be grateful for your assistance.
RODAS. Well, find someone else to give it them. I'm resting here.

(*The* VILLAGERS *laugh*)

PIZARRO. Rest. (*To young Martin*) Who's this?
DIEGO. Martin Ruiz, sir. He's a good boy. He knows all his codes of Chivalry by heart, and he's aching to be a page, sir.
PIZARRO. How old?
YOUNG MARTIN. Seventeen.
PIZARRO. Don't lie.
OLD MARTIN. Fifteen, sir.

(OLD MARTIN *exits*)

PIZARRO. Parents?
YOUNG MARTIN. Dead, sir.
PIZARRO. Can you write?
YOUNG MARTIN. Two hundred Latin words. Three hundred Spanish.

Pizarro. Why do you want to come, Martin?

Young Martin. It's going to be glorious, sir.

Pizarro. Look, you, if you served me you'd be page to an old slogger; no titles, no traditions. I learnt my trade as a mercenary, going with who best paid me. It's a closed book to me, all that chivalry. But then, not reading or writing, all books are closed to me. If I took you, you'd have to be my reader and writer, both.

Young Martin. I'd be honoured, my Lord. Oh, please, my Lord!

Pizarro. General will do. Let's see your respect. Greet me.

(Young Martin *bows. The* Villagers *laugh*)

Now to the Church. That's Brother Valverde, our Chaplain.

Valverde. The blessing of God on you, my son. And on all who come with us to alter the heathen.

Pizarro. Now to our Second-in-Command, Cavalier de Soto. I'm sure you all know the Cavalier well by reputation; a great soldier. He has served under Cordoba! No expedition he seconds can fail.

(Rodas *makes a derisive noise.* Pizarro *takes a roll of cloth, woven with the design of a llama, from De Soto and shakes it out*)

Now look at this! Indian stuff! Ten years ago, standing with the great Balboa, I saw a chieftain draw this beast on the leaf of an aloe. And he said to me: 'Where this roams is uncountable wealth!'

Rodas. Oh yes, pissing uncountable! You ask Sanchez the farrier about that. He listened to tales like that from him five years ago.

Diego. Who cares about him?

Rodas. Uncountable bloody wealth? It rained for six months and his skin rotted on him. They lost twenty-seven out of fifty.

Pizarro. And so we may again. (*To Rodas; slowly*) What do you think I'm offering you? A walk in the country? Wines and jellies in a basket, your hand round your girl? No, I'm promising you swamps. Steaming jungle. Sitting half the day buried in earth to escape the mouths of insects. You may live for weeks on palm tree-buds and soup boiled out of leather straps. And at night you will sleep in thick wet darkness with snakes hung over your heads like bell-ropes—and black men under bushes, waiting—men that eat each other. And why should you endure all this? Because I believe that beyond this terrible place is a kingdom where gold is as common as wood is here, or as iron is in Biscay. I took only two steps in and found cups and pans made out of it solid.

(*The* Villagers *laugh and start to exit.* Pizarro *claps his hands twice.* Felipillo *enters. The* Villagers *stop.* Felipillo *is a slim, delicate Indian from Ecuador, loaded with golden ornaments. In actuality,* Felipillo *is a treacherous and hysterical creature, but at the moment, under his master's eye, he sways forward before the stupefied villagers with a demure grace*)

I present Felipillo, captured on my last trip. Look close at his ornaments. To him they are no more than feathers are to us, but they are all gold, my friends. Down. Examine him.

(*The* Villagers *move to* Felipillo *and examine him*)

Valverde. Look at him well, my sons! This is a heathen—a being condemned to eternal flame unless you help him. (*He turns to Pizarro*) Don't think we are merely going to destroy his people and lift their wealth. We are going to take from them what they don't value, and give them instead the priceless mercy of heaven. He who helps me lift this dark man into light, I absolve of all crimes he ever committed.

Pizarro. Well?

Salinas. That's gold right enough.

Pizarro. And for your taking. (*To the Villagers*) I was like you once. Sitting the afternoon away in this same street, drunk in the inn, to bed in the sty. Stink and mud and nothing to live for. Even if you die with me, what's so tender-precious to hold you here?

Vasca. You're pissing right!

Pizarro. I tell you—over there you'll be the masters and that'll be your slave.

Vasca. There's a thought: talk about the slave of slaves! (*He makes the sign of the cross*)

Domingo (*timidly*) Do you think it's true?

Pizarro. Do you say I lie?

Domingo. Oh no, sir . . .

Vasca. Even if he does, what's to keep you here? You're a cooper: how many casks have you made in the last year? That's no employment for a pissing dog.

Pizarro. Well, what d'you say?

Juan. I say right, sir!

Vasca. Me, too. I'm going to get a slave or two like him!

Domingo. Yes. Vasca's right; you can't do worse than stay here.

Rodas. Well, not me, boys. You won't catch Rodas marching through no pissing jungle.

Salinas. Oh, shut your ape's face. (*To Pizarro*) He'll come, sir.

(*The* Villagers *cheer*)

Pizarro. All right, then! Diego, make your way to Toledo for the muster. Enrol them all and take them along.

Diego. Sir!

(*The* Villagers *exit.* Young Martin *starts to exit in the opposite direction.* Pizarro *stays him*)

Pizarro. Boy. (*He holds out his arms for his cloak to be taken off*)

(*There is a pause, then* Young Martin *takes off the cloak*)

Master me the names of all officers and men so far listed.
YOUNG MARTIN (*bowing*) Yes, sir!
PIZARRO. You're a page now, so act like one. Dignity at all times.
YOUNG MARTIN (*bowing*) Yes, sir.
PIZARRO. Respect.
YOUNG MARTIN (*bowing*) Yes, sir.
PIZARRO. Obedience.
YOUNG MARTIN (*bowing*) Yes, sir.
PIZARRO. And there's no need to salute every ten seconds.
YOUNG MARTIN. No, sir.
VALVERDE (*smiling*) Come, my son, there's work to be done.

(*There is a pause.* YOUNG MARTIN *stares adoringly at Pizarro, then runs off.* VALVERDE *follows*)

PIZARRO. Strange sight, Yourself, just as you were in this very street.
DE SOTO. Do you like it?
PIZARRO. No, I was a fool. Dreamers deserve what they get.
DE SOTO. And what are you dreaming now?
PIZARRO. Gold.
DE SOTO. Oh, come. Gold is not enough loadstone for you, not any more, to drag you back to the new world.
PIZARRO. You're right. At my age things become what they really are. Gold turns into metal.
DE SOTO. Then why? You could stay here now and be a hero for a province. What's left to endure so much for—especially with your infirmity? You've earned the right to comfort. Your country would gladly grant it to you for the rest of your life.
PIZARRO. My country. Where's that? My country?
DE SOTO. Spain, sir.

PIZARRO. Spain and I have been strangers since I was a boy. The only spot I know in it is here—this filthy village. This is Spain to me. Is this where you wish me comfort? For twenty-two years I drove pigs down this street because my father couldn't own my mother. Twenty-two years without one single day of hope. And when I finally turned soldier and dragged my arquebus along the roads of Italy, I was so famined I was beyond eating. I got nothing and I gave nothing. And though I groaned for that once, I'm glad with it now. Because I owe nothing. Once the world could have had me for a pretty farm, two rocky fields and a Señor to my name. It said 'No'. Ten years on, it could have had me for double—small estates, fifty oranges and a Sir to them. It said 'No'. Twenty years more, it could still have had me cheap; Balboa's trusty lieutenant, marched with him to the Pacific and claimed it for Spain: state pension and dinner once a week with the local mayor. But the world said 'No'. Said 'No' and said 'No'. Well, now it's going to know me. If I live this next year I'm going to get me a name that won't ever be forgotten. A

name to be sung here for centuries in your ballads, out there under
the cork trees where I sat as a boy with bandages for shoes. I amuse
you.

DE SOTO. Surely you see you don't.

PIZARRO. Oh yes, I amuse you, Cavalier de Soto. The old pig-herd
lumbering after fame. You inherited your honour—I have to root for
mine like the pigs. It's amusing.

(The LIGHTS *become whiter, colder.* PIZARRO *kneels. An*   **Scene ii**
organ sounds—the austere polyphony of Spanish celebration.   **Effects**
VALVERDE *enters, bearing an immense wooden Christ. He is*   **cue 1**
accompanied by his assistant, FRAY MARCOS DE NIZZA, *a*
Franciscan, a man of far more serene temper and intellectual   **Light**
maturity. All the VILLAGERS *enter, wearing the white cloaks*   **cue 3**
of chivalry and carrying banners. Among them is PEDRO DE CANDIA, *a*
Venetian captain, wearing a pearl in one ear and walking with a lazy
stealth that at once suggests danger. OLD MARTIN *enters apart from the*
others, and speaks out front)

OLD MARTIN. On the day of St John the Evangelist,   **Effects**
our banners were consecrated in the Cathedral Church   **cue 2**
of Panama. Our muster was one hundred and eighty-
seven, with horses for twenty-seven.

VALVERDE *(to the assembly)* You are the hunstmen of God. The
weapons you draw are sacred. Oh God, invest us all with the courage
of Thy unflinching Son. Show us the way to beat the savage out of
his dark forests on to the broad plain of Thy Grace.

DE NIZZA. And comfort, we pray, all warriors that shall be in
affliction from this setting out.

OLD MARTIN *(indicating* DE NIZZA) Fray Marcos de Nizza,
Franciscan, appointed to assist Valverde.

DE NIZZA. You are the bringers of food to starving peoples. You
go to break mercy with them like bread, and pour out gentleness
into their cups. You will lay before them the inexhaustible table of
free spirit, and invite to it all who have dieted on terror. You will
bring to all tribes the nourishment of pity. You will sow their fields
with love, and teach them to harvest the crop of it, each yield in its
season. Remember this always—we are their New World.

VALVERDE. Approach, all, and be blessed.

(During the following, the MEN *kneel and are blessed, afterwards*
rising again)

OLD MARTIN *(indicating)* Pedro de Candia, Cavalier from Venice,
in charge of weapons and artillery. These villagers you know already.
There were many others, of course. Almagro, the General's partner,
who stayed to organize reinforcements and follow in three months.
Riquelme, the Treasurer. Pedro of Ayala and Blas of Atienza.
Herrada the Swordsman and Golzales of Toledo. And Juan de

Barbaran whom everyone called the good servant out of love for him. And many smaller men. Even its youngest member saw himself with a following of Indians and a province for an orchard. It was a tumbled company, none too noble, but ginger for wealth.

(ESTETE *enters, a stiff and haughty man, dressed in the*   **Effects**
black of the Spanish Court)   **cue 3**

And chiefly there was . . .

ESTETE. Miguel Estete. Royal Veedor, and Overseer in the name of King Carlos the Fifth. You should not have allowed anyone to be blessed before me.

PIZARRO. Your pardon, Veedor. I do not understand affairs of before and after.

ESTETE. That is evident. General, on this expedition my word is the law: it is spoken with the King's authority.

PIZARRO. Your pardon, but on this expedition *my* word is the law: there will be no other.

ESTETE. In matters military.

PIZARRO. In all matters.

ESTETE. In all that do not infringe the majesty of the King.

PIZARRO. What matters could?

ESTETE. Remember your duty to God, sir, and to the throne, sir, and you will not discover them. Continue!

PIZARRO (*furious*) De Soto! In the name of Spain our holy country, I invest you as second-in-command to me. Subject only to me. In the name of Spain our holy country, I—I . . . (*He falters, clutching his side in pain*)

(*There is a pause. The* MEN *whisper among themselves*)

DE CANDIA. Be still!

PIZARRO. Take the banners out . . .   **Effects cue 4**

DE SOTO (*commanding*) Take up your banners. March!   **Light cue 4**

(*The organ music continues.* ALL *march out, leaving* PIZARRO *and* YOUNG MARTIN *alone on the stage. Only when all the rest are gone does* PIZARRO *collapse.* YOUNG MARTIN *is frightened and concerned*)   **Effects cue 5**

YOUNG MARTIN. What is it, sir?   **Effects cue 6**

PIZARRO. A wound from long ago. A knife cut to the bone. A savage put it into me for life. It troubles me at times. You'll start long before me with your wounds. With your killing, too. I wonder how you'll like that.

YOUNG MARTIN. You watch me, sir.

PIZARRO. I will. You deal in deaths when you are a soldier, and all your study should be to make them clean, what scratches kill and how to cut them.

YOUNG MARTIN. But surely, sir, there's more to soldiering than that?

PIZARRO. You mean honour, glory—traditions of the service?

YOUNG MARTIN. Yes, sir.

PIZARRO. Dungballs. Soldiers are for killing; that's their reason.

YOUNG MARTIN. But, sir . . .

PIZARRO. What?

YOUNG MARTIN. It's not just killing.

PIZARRO. Listen, Martin: know something. Men cannot just stand as men in this world. It's too big for them and they grow scared. So they build themselves shelters against the bigness. They call the shelters Army, Court, Church. Well, they're useful against loneliness, Martin, useful—but they're not real, they're not true, Martin. Do you see?

YOUNG MARTIN. No, sir. Not truthfully, sir . . .

PIZARRO. No, sir. Not truthfully, sir! Why must you be so young? Look at you. A colt the world will break for its sightless track. Listen once. The world of soldiers is a yard of ungrowable children. They play with ribbons and make up ceremonies just to keep out the rest of the world. They add up the number of their blue dead and their green dead and call that their history. But all this is just the flower the bandit carves on his knife before shoving it into a man's side. What's Army tradition—this great tradition you hear of? Nothing but years of Us against Them. Christ-men against Pagan-men. Men against men. I've had a life of it, boy, and let me tell you that it's nothing but a nightmare's game, played by brutes to give themselves a meaning.

YOUNG MARTIN. But, sir, a noble reason can make a fight glorious.

PIZARRO. Give me one reason that stays noble once you start hacking off limbs in its name. There isn't a cause in the world to set against this pain. Noble's a word, Martin. Leave it for the books.

YOUNG MARTIN. I can't believe that, sir.

PIZARRO. Look at you. Hope, lovely hope, it's on you like dew. Do you know where you're going? Into the forest. A hundred miles of dark and screaming. The dark we all came out of, hot. Things flying, fleeing, falling dead—and their death unnoticed. Take your noble reasons there, Martin. Pitch your silk flags in that black and wave your crosses at the wild cats. See what awe they command. Be advised, boy. Go back to Spain.

YOUNG MARTIN. No, sir. I'm coming with you. I can learn, sir.

PIZARRO. You will be taught, Not by me. By the forest.   **Effects cue 7**

(PIZARRO *exits.* YOUNG MARTIN *is left alone. The*   **Scene iii**
stage darkens and the huge medallion high on the back wall   **Light**
begins to glow. Great cries of 'Inca' are heard. YOUNG   **cue 5**
MARTIN *bolts off the stage. Exotic music mixes with the chanting. Slowly the medallion opens out to form a huge golden sun with twelve great rays. In the centre stands* ATAHUALLPA, *sovereign Inca of Peru, masked, crowned, and dressed in gold. When he speaks, his voice, and the voices of all the Incas, is strangely formalized.* VILLAC UMU, *the high priest,*

CHALLCUCHIMA, MANCO *and others, all masked, and robed in terracotta,
enter below the Inca court. They prostrate themselves*)

VILLAC UMU. Atahuallpa! God!
ATAHUALLPA. God hears.
MANCO. Manco your Chasqui speaks. I bring truth from many
runners what has been seen in the Farthest Province. White men
sitting on huge sheep. The sheep are red! Everywhere their leader
shouts aloud: 'Here is God."
ATAHUALLPA. The White God!
VILLAC UMU. Beware.
CHALLCUCHIMA. Beware, Inca!
ATAHUALLPA. All-powerful spirit who left this place before my
ancestors ruled you. The White God returns!
CHALLCUCHIMA. You do not know this.
ATAHUALLPA. He has long been waited for. If he comes, it is with
blessing. Then my people will see I did well to take the Crown.
VILLAC UMU. Beware, beware, Inca. Your Mother Moon wears
a veil of green fire. An eagle fell on to the temple in Cuzco.
MANCO. It is true, Capac. He fell out of the sky.
VILLAC UMU. Out of a green sky.
CHALLCUCHIMA. On to a house of gold.
VILLAC UMU. When the world ends, small birds grow sharp claws.
ATAHUALLPA. Cover your mouth.

(ALL *cover their mouths*)

If the White God comes to bless me, all must see him.   **Light
                                                                cue 6**

(*The* COURT *retires.* ATAHUALLPA *remains on the stage,*   **Effects
motionless in his sunflower. He stays in this position until the   cue 8**
end of Scene vii.*

    The Province of Tumbes. The LIGHTS *become mottled,*   **Scene iv
suggesting a forest. Screams and whoops of alarm are heard,*   Effects
imitating tropical bird cries. A horde of* INDIANS *rushes   cue 9**
across the stage, pursued by* SOLDIERS, PIZARRO, DE CANDIA,
DE SOTO, VALVERDE, ESTETE *and* FELIPILLO)

DE CANDIA. Grab that one! That's the chief.

(*The* SOLDIERS *capture the* CHIEFTAIN. *At the sight of this, all the*
INDIANS *fall silent and passive.* DE CANDIA *approaches them with
drawn sword*)

Now, you brownie bastard, show us gold.
PIZARRA. Gently, De Candia. You'll get nothing from him in
terror.
DE CANDIA. Let's see.
PIZARRO. Put up! God's bread . . . Felipillo, ask for gold.

(FELIPILLO *adopts a set of stylized gestures for his interpreting, in the manner of sign language*)

CHIEF. We have no gold. All was taken by the great King in his war.

PIZARRO. What king?

CHIEF. Holy Atahuallpa.

INDIANS (*chanting*) Ata-huallpa.

CHIEF. Inca of earth and sky. His kingdom is the widest in the world.

DE SOTO. How wide?

CHIEF. A man can run in it every day for a year.

DE SOTO. More than a thousand miles.

ESTETE. Poor savage, trying to impress us with his little tribe.

PIZARRO. I think we've found more than a little tribe, Veedor. (*To the Chief*) Tell me of this King. Who did he fight?

CHIEF. His brother Huascar. His father the great Inca Hyayana grew two sons. One by a wife, one by a not-wife. At his death he cut the Kingdom in two for them. But Atahuallpa wanted all. So he made war, and killed his brother. Now he is lord of earth and sky.

PIZARRO. And he's the bastard?

(*All the* INDIANS *cry out:* 'Ka-way-ya!')

Answer! He's the bastard?

CHIEF. He is the Son of the Sun. He needs no wedded mother. He is God.

INDIANS (*chanting*) Sapa! Inca! Inca! Capac!

PIZARRO. God?

CHIEF. God!

PIZARRO. God on earth?

DE SOTO. Do you believe this?

CHIEF. It is true. The sun is God. Atahuallpa is his child sent to shine on us for a few years of life. Then he will return to his father's palace and live for ever.

PIZARRO. God on earth?

VALVERDE. Oh, my brothers, where have we come? The land of Anti-Christ! Do your duty, Spaniards! Take each an Indian and work to shift his soul. (*He shows the cross to the Indians*) The cross, you pagan dust!

(*The* INDIANS *try to escape*)

Stay them!

(*The* SPANIARDS *ring the Indians with swords*)

Down! Repeat after me. Jesus Christ Inca!

(FELIPILLO *interprets*)

INDIANS (*uncertainly*) Jesus Christ Inca!

VALVERDE. Jesus Christ Inca!

ESTETE (*moving to the Chief*) Jesus Christ Inca . . . (*He kicks the Chief*)

(*The* CHIEF *runs across the stage and leads the* INDIANS *off. The* SOLDIERS *herd them away. Their cries punctuate the end of the scene.* ALL *exit except* PIZARRO *and* DE SOTO)

ATAHUALLPA (*at the fourth 'Jesus Christ Inca'*) He surely is a God! He teaches my people to praise him!

PIZARRO. He's a God all right. They're scared to hell of him. And a bastard, too. That's civil war—bastards against bastards!

ATAHUALLPA. I will see him. Let no one harm these men!

PIZARRO. Let's see you, then! What's it like to be Son of the Sun?

DE SOTO. That's something in Europe no one's ever dared to call himself.

PIZARRO. God on earth, living for ever!

DE SOTO. He's got a shock coming!

(DE SOTO *exits*)

PIZARRO. Did you hear that, God? You're not going to like that! Because we've got a God worth a thousand of you. A gentle God with gentle priests, and a couple of big cannon to blow you out of the sky!

VALVERDE (*off*) Jesus Christ Inca!

PIZARRO. Christ the Merciful with his shackles and stakes! So you enjoy yourself while you can. Have yourself a glorious shine! (*He makes the sign of the cross with his sword*) Take *that*, Anti-Christ!

Effects
cue 10

(PIZARRO *runs off, laughing*)

ESTETE (*off*) Jesus Christ Inca!

INDIANS (*off*) Jesus—Christ—Inca!

Light
cue 7

(VILLAC UMU *and* CHALLCUCHIMA *enter*)

VILLAC UMU (*to Atahuallpa*) Your people groan.

ATAHUALLPA. They groan with my voice!

CHALLCUCHIMA (*to Atahuallpa*) Your people weep.

ATAHUALLPA. They weep with my tears!

CHALLCUCHIMA. He searches all the houses. He seeks your crown. Remember the prophecy! The twelfth Lord of the Four Quarters shall be the last. Inca, beware!

VILLAC UMU. Ware, Inca.

CHALLCUCHIMA. Ware!

ATAHUALLPA (*to Challcuchima*) Go to him. Take him my word. Tell him to greet me at Cajamarca, behind the great mountains. If he is a God, he will find me. If he is no God—he will die!

Effects
cue 11

(*The* LIGHTS *go down on the Sun.* VILLAC UMU *and*   **Scene v**
CHALLCUCHIMA *exit.*   **Light**
     cue 8

Night. Wild bird cries are heard. DOMINGO *and* VASCA
enter on sentry duty)

VASCA. There must be a bloody thousand of 'em, every
night we halt.
DOMINGO. Why don't they just come and get us?
VASCA. They're waiting.
DOMINGO. What for?
VASCA. Maybe they're cannibals and there's a feast day coming
up.
DOMINGO. Very funny. Six weeks in this pissing forest and not one
smell of gold. I think we've been had.
VASCA. Unless they're hiding it, like the General says.
DOMINGO. I don't believe it. God-damned place. I'm even starting
to rust.
VASCA. We all are. It's the damp. Another week and   **Effects**
we'll have to get the blacksmith to cut us out.   **cue 12**

(ESTETE *enters with* DE CANDIA *carrying an arquebus*)

VASCA   ⎫
         ⎬ (*together*) Who's there?
DOMINGO ⎭
DE CANDIA. You talk on duty again and *I'll* cut you   **Effects**
out.   **cue 13**
DOMINGO. Yes, sir.
VASCA. Yes, sir.

(DOMINGO *and* VASCA *separate and exit*)

DE CANDIA. They're right. Everything's rusting. (*To the gun*) Even
you, my darling. What sacrilege. Strozzi's most perfect
model. She can stop a horse at five hundred paces. You're   **Effects**
too good for brownies, my sweet.   **cue 14**
ESTETE. What are they waiting for? Why don't they
just attack and be done with it?
DE CANDIA. They'd find nothing against them. A hundred and
eighty terrified men, nine of these and two cannon. If your King
wasn't so mean we might just have a chance here.
ESTETE. Hold your tongue, De Candia.
DE CANDIA. Ah, good. Loyalty: that's what I like to see. You
puzzle me, Veedor. What do you get out of this? They tell me
Royal Overseers get nothing.
ESTETE. Any man without self-interest must puzzle a Venetian.
If you serve a king you must kill personal ambition. Only then can
you become a channel between the people and its col-   **Effects**
lective glory—which otherwise it would never feel. In   **cue 15**
Byzantium court officials were castrated to resemble the
Order of Angels. But I don't expect *you* to understand.

De Candia. You Spaniards! You men with missions!
You just can't bear to think of yourselves as the thieves
you are.

Estete. How dare you, sir!

*Effects
cue 16*

(*There is a loud burst of bird cries.* Pizarro *and* Young Martin
enter upstage)

De Candia. Our noble General. They say in the Indies he traded
his immortal part to the Devil.

Estete. What for, pray? Health? Breeding? Handsomeness?

De Candia. That they don't tell.

Estete. I dare say not. I only wonder His Majesty could give
command to such a man. You know that he can neither read nor
write. I believe he's mad.

De Candia. No, but still dangerous.

Estete. What do you mean?

De Candia. I've served many men: but this is the
first who makes me afraid. Look into him, you'll see a
kind of death.

*Effects
cue 17
Effects
cue 18*

(De Candia *and* Estete *move upstage as* Pizarro *and* Young
Martin *come down. Bird cries fill the forest*)

Pizarro. Listen, Martin, listen to them. There's the
world. The eagle rips the condor: the condor rips the
crow. And the crow would blind all the eagles in the sky
if once it had the beak to do it. The clothed hunt the
naked; the legitimate hunt the bastards, and put down
the word Gentleman to blot up the blood. Your chivalry
laws don't govern me, Martin. They're for belonging
birds—like *them*: legitimate birds with claws trim on the
perch their fathers left them. Make no error. If once I
could peck them off it, I'd tear them into gobbets to feed
cats. Don't ever trust me, boy.

*Effects
cue 19

Effects
cue 20

Effects
cue 21

Effects
cue 22

Effects
cue 23*

Young Martin. Sir? I'm your man.

Pizarro. Don't ever trust me. Or if you must, never say I
deceived you. Know me.

Young Martin. I do, sir. You are all I ever want to be.

Pizarro. I am nothing you could ever want to be, or any man
alive. Believe this: if the time ever came when you harried me, I'd
rip you too, easy as look at you. Because *you* belong too, Martin.

Young Martin. I belong to *you*, sir!

Pizarro. No. You belong to hope. To faith. To priests and
pretences. To dipping flags and ducking heads; to laying hands and
licking rings; to powers and parchments; and the whole vast stupid
congregation of crowners and cross-kissers. You're a worshipper,
Martin. A groveller. You were born with feet but you·prefer your

knees. It's you who make kings—bishops—generals. You trust me, I'll hurt you past believing. (*He pauses*) Have the sentries changed? **Effects** cue 24 **Effects** cue 25

YOUNG MARTIN (*sulkily*) Not yet, sir.

PIZARRO. Little Lord of Hope, I'm harsh with you. You own everything I've lost. I despise the keeping, and I loathe the losing. Where can a man stand, between two hates? (*He moves up to the two others*) De Candia! Estete! **Effects** cue 26

ESTETE. General. How is your wound tonight? **Effects** cue 27

PIZARRO. The calmer for your inquiring, Veedor.

ESTETE. Well, and what's your plan, sir?

PIZARRO. To go on until I'm stopped.

DE CANDIA. Admirable simplicity, General.

ESTETE. What kind of plan is that?

PIZARRO. You have a better? It's obvious they've been ordered to hold off.

ESTETE. Why, pray?

PIZARRO. Well, if it's wickedness, I'm sure the Crown can guess it as soon as the Army.

ESTETE. Sir, I know your birth hasn't fitted you for much civility, but remember, in me speaks your King.

PIZARRO. Well, go and write to him. That's the skill you're proud of, isn't it—writing? Set down more about my unfitness in your report. Then show it to the birds. **Effects** cue 28

(PIZARRO *exits followed by* YOUNG MARTIN. ESTETE *exits the opposite way, followed by* DE CANDIA *laughing.*)

The LIGHTS *brighten to morning.* OLD MARTIN *enters*) **Scene vi** **Light** cue 9 **Effects** cue 29 **Effects** cue 30

OLD MARTIN. We were in the forest for six weeks, but at last we escaped and found on the other side our first witness of a great empire. There was a road fifteen feet wide, bordered with mimosa and blue glories, with walls on both sides the height of a man. We rode it for days, six horses abreast: and all the way, far up the hillsides, were huge fields of corn, laid out in terraces, and a net of water in a thousand canals.

(OLD MARTIN *exits.* MANCO *enters*)

MANCO. Manco your Chasqui speaks. They move on the road to Ricaplaya. **Light** cue 10

ATAHUALLPA. What do they do?

MANCO. They walk through the field terraces. They listen to toil-songs. They clap their hands at fields of llama!

(*Groups of* INDIANS *enter, singing a toil-song and miming their work of sowing and reaping.* PIZARRO, *the* PRIESTS, FELIPILLO *and* SOLDIERS, *among them* DE SOTO, DE CANDIA, DIEGO, ESTETE *and* YOUNG

MARTIN, *enter and stand watching.* YOUNG MARTIN *carries a drum*)

Light
cue II

DE NIZZA. How beautiful their tongue sounds.

YOUNG MARTIN. It's very hard. I'm trying to study it, but all the words seem to slip together.

FELIPILLO. Oh, very hard, yes. But more hard for Indian to learn Spanish.

DE NIZZA. I'm sure. See how contented they look. This could be Eden at the world's start. When work was praise, and vegetables sang.

DIEGO. It's the first time I've ever seen people happy at working. Look!

DE SOTO (*indicating the Headman of the Indians*) That is their Headman.

PIZARRO. You are the Lord of the Manor?

(FELIPILLO *interprets*)

HEADMAN. Here all work together in families: fifty, a hundred, a thousand. I am head of a thousand families. I give out to all food. I give out to all clothes. I give out to all confessing.

DE NIZZA. Confessing? You have confessing?

HEADMAN. I have priest power. I confess my people of all crimes against the laws of the sun.

DE SOTO. What laws are there?

HEADMAN. It is the seventh month. That is why they must pick corn.

ATAHUALLPA (*intoning*) In the eighth month you will plough. In the ninth, sow maize. In the tenth, mend your roofs.

HEADMAN. Each age also has its tasks.

ATAHUALLPA. Nine years to twelve, protect harvests. Twelve to eighteen, care for herds. Eighteen to twenty-five—warriors for *me*—Atahuallpa Inca!

FELIPILLO. They are stupid! Always do what they are told.

DE SOTO. This is because they are poor?

FELIPILLO. Not poor. Not rich. All same.

ATAHUALLPA. At twenty-five all will marry. All will receive one tupu of land.

HEADMAN. What may be covered by one hundred pounds of maize.

ATAHUALLPA. They will never move from there. At birth of a son, one more tupu will be given. At birth of a daughter, *half* a tupu. At fifty all people will leave work for ever, and be fed in honour till they die.

DE SOTO. I have settled several lands. This is the first I've entered which shames our Spain.

ESTETE. Shames?

PIZARRO. Oh, it's not difficult to shame Spain. But here shames every country which teaches we are born greedy for possessions. Clearly we're made greedy when we're assured it's natural. But there's a picture for the Spanish eye! There's nothing to covet, so coveting dies at birth.

DE SOTO. But don't you have any nobles or grand people?

HEADMAN. The King has great men near him to order the country. But they are few.

DE SOTO. How, then, can he be sure so many are happy over so large a land?

HEADMAN. His messengers run light and dark, one after one, over four great roads. No one else may move on them. So he has eyes everywhere. He sees you now. **Effects cue 31**

PIZARRO. Now?

ATAHUALLPA. Now! **Light cue 12**

(*Music is heard.* CHALLCUCHIMA *enters with* MANCO, *bearing the image of the Sun on a pole*)

CHALLCUCHIMA. You see Challcuchima, High General of the Sun. I bring greetings from Atahuallpa Inca, Lord of the Four Quarters, King of the earth and sky.

ESTETE. I will speak with him. A King's man must always greet a King's man. We bring greetings from King Carlos, Emperor of Spain and Austria. We bring blessing from Jesus Christ, the Son of God.

ATAHUALLPA. Blessing!

CHALLCUCHIMA. *I* am sent by the son of God. He orders *you* to visit him.

ESTETE. Orders? Does he take us for servants?

CHALLCUCHIMA. All men are his servants.

ESTETE. Does he think so? He's got awakening coming.

CHALLCUCHIMA. Awakening?

PIZARRO. Veedor, under pardon, let my thick peasant tongue have a word. (*To Challcuchima*) Where is your King?

CHALLCUCHIMA. Cajamarca. Behind the great mountains. Perhaps they are too high for you.

ESTETE. There isn't a hill in your whole country a Spaniard couldn't climb in full armour.

CHALLCUCHIMA. That is wonderful.

PIZARRO. God's bread, Veedor! (*To Challcuchima*) How long should we march before we find him?

CHALLCUCHIMA. One life of Mother Moon.

FELIPILLO. A month.

PIZARRO. For us, two weeks! Tell him we come!

(*There is general reaction*)

ATAHUALLPA. He gives his word with no fear.

CHALLCUCHIMA. Ware you! It is great danger to take back your word.

PIZARRO. I do not fear danger. What I say I do.   **Effects**
CHALLCUCHIMA (*turning*) So. Do.   **cue 32**

(CHALLCUCHIMA *and* MANCO *stalk off*)

ATAHUALLPA. He speaks with a God's tongue. Let us take his
blessing!
DE SOTO. Well, God help us now!
DE CANDIA. He'd better. I don't know who else will get us out of
this. Certainly not the artillery!
FELIPILLO (*imitating Challcuchima's walk and voice*) So! Do!
DE SOTO. Be still. You're too free.
ESTETE. My advice to you now is to wait for the reinforcements.
PIZARRO. I thank you for it. Superb counsel, Veedor.
DE SOTO. There's no telling when they'll come, sir. We daren't
wait till then.
PIZARRO (*to Estete*) But *you* of course will.
ESTÉTE. I?
PIZARRO. I cannot hazard the life of a Royal officer.
ESTETE. My personal safety has never concerned me, General.
My master's service is all I care for.
PIZARRO. That's why we must ensure its continuance. I'll give
you twenty men. You can make a garrison.
ESTETE. I must decline, General. If you go—I go also.
PIZARRO. I'm infinitely moved, Veedor—but my orders remain.
You stay here. (*To Young Martin*) Call Assembly.
YOUNG MARTIN (*banging his drum*) Assembly!   **Light**
Assembly!   **cue 13**

(*The* COMPANY *pelts on.* ESTETE *exits angrily*)   **Scene vii**

PIZARRO. We are commanded to Court by a brown
King, more powerful than any you have ever heard of, sole owner of
all the gold we came for. We have three roads. Go back, and he kills
us. Stay here, and he kills us. Go on, and he still may kill us. Who
fears to meet him can stay here with the Veedor and swell a garrison. He'll have no disgrace, but no gold neither. Who stirs?
RODAS. Well, I pissing stir for once. I'm not going to be chewed
up by no bloody heathen king. What do you say, Vasca lad?
VASCA. I don't know. I reckon if he chews us first, he chews you
second. We're the eggs and you're the stew.
RODAS. Ha, ha, day of a hundred jokes!
SALINAS. Come on, friend, for God's sake. Who's going to sew us
up if you desert?
RODAS. You can all rot for all I care, breeches and what's bloody
in 'em.
SALINAS. Bastard!
RODAS. To hell with the lot of you!

(RODAS *exits*)

PIZARRO. Anyone else?

DOMINGO. Well, I don't know—maybe he's right.

JUAN. Hey, Pedro, what do you think?

PEDRO. Hell, no! Vasca's right. It's as safe to go as to stay here.

SALINAS. Bloody right!

VASCA. Anyway, I didn't come to keep no pissing garrison.

PEDRO. Nor me. I'm going on.

JUAN. Right, boy.

SALINAS. And me.

DOMINGO. Well, I don't know . . .

VASCA. Oh, close your mouth. You're like a pissing girl. (*To Pizarro*) We're coming. Just find us the gold.

PIZARRO. All right then. (*To Young Martin*) You stay here.

YOUNG MARTIN. No, sir. The place of a squire is at all times by his knight's side. Laws of Chivalry.

PIZARRO (*touched*) Get them in rank. *Move!*

YOUNG MARTIN. Company in rank. Move!

(*The* SOLDIERS *form up in rank*)

PIZARRO. Stand firm. Firmer! Look at you; you could be dead already. If he sees you like that you will be. Make no error, he's watching every step you take. You're not men any longer, you're gods now. Eternal gods, each one of you. Two can play this immortality game, my lads. I want to see you move over this land like figures from a Lent Procession. He must see Gods walk on earth. Indifferent! Uncrushable! No death to be afraid of. I tell you, one shiver dooms the lot of us. One yelp of fright and we'll never be heard of again. He'll serve us like cheese-worms you crush with a knife. So come on, you tattered trash—shake out the straw. Forget your village magics: fingers in crosses, saints under your shirts. You can grant prayers now—no need to offer them. Come on! Fix your eyes! Follow the pig-boy to his glory! I'll have an Empire for my farm. A million boys driving in the pigs at night. And each one of you will own a share—juicy black earth a hundred mile apiece— and golden ploughs to slice it! Get up, you god-boys. **Light** March! **cue 14**

(YOUNG MARTIN *bangs his drum. The* SPANIARDS *begin to march in slow motion. Above, masked* INDIANS *move on to the upper level,* MANCO, CHALLCUCHIMA *and* VILLAC UMU *among them*)

MANCO. They move, Inca. They come! One hundred and sixty-seven.

ATAHUALLPA. Where?

MANCO. Zaran.

VILLAC UMU. Beware! Beware, Inca!

MANCO. They move all in step. Not fast, not slow. They keep straight on from dark to dark.

VILLAC UMU. Beware! Beware, Inca!
MANCO. They are at Motupe, Inca! They do not look on left or
right.
VILLAC UMU. Beware! This is great danger.
ATAHUALLPA. No danger. He is coming to bless me.   **Effects**
A God and all his priests. Praise Father Sun!   **cue 33**
ALL ABOVE (*chanting*) Vivacocha! Atix!
ATAHUALLPA (*chanting*) Praise Sapa Inca!
ALL ABOVE (*chanting*) Sapa Inca! Inca Capac!
ATAHUALLPA (*chanting*) Praise Inti Cori.
ALL ABOVE (*chanting*) Keild Ya, Inti Cori!
MANCO. They come to the mountains.
VILLAC UMU. Kill them now.
ATAHUALLPA (*chanting*) Praise Atahuallpa!
CHALLCUCHIMA. Destroy them! Teach them death!
ATAHUALLPA (*chanting*) *Praise Atahuallpa!*
ALL ABOVE (*chanting*) Atahuallpa! Sapa Inca! Hua-car-cu-ya-t!

ATAHUALLPA (*crying out*) Let them see my mountains!   **Light**
                                          cue 15
   (*There is a crash of primitive instruments. The lights
snap out and, lit from the side, the rays of the metal sun throw long
shadows across the wooden wall. All the* SPANIARDS *fall down. A cold
blue light fills the stage*)

(OLD MARTIN *enters below*)

OLD MARTIN. You call them the Andes. Picture a curtain of stone
hung by some giant across your path. Mountains set on mountains;
cliffs on cliffs. Hands of rock a hundred yards high, with flashing
nails where the snow never moved, scratching the gashed face of the
sun. For miles around us the jungle lay black in its shadow. A freezing
cold fell on us.
PIZARRO. Up, my godlings. Up, my little gods. Take heart now.
He's watching you. *Get to your feet.*

(*The* SPANIARDS *rise*)

(*To Diego*) What of the horses?
DIEGO. D'you need them, sir?
PIZARRO. They're vital, boy.
DIEGO. Then you will have 'em, sir. They'll follow you as we will.

   (*During the following speech* ATAHUALLPA *beckons thrice to Pizarro,
and retires backwards out of the sun into blackness*)

PIZARRO. Up we go, then! Atahuallpa, I'm coming for you. Show
me the toppest peak-top you can pile—show me the lid of the world
—I'll stand tiptoe on it and pull you out of the sky, you Son of the

Sun. I'll grab you by the legs and smash your flaming crown on the
rocks. Bless them, Church!

VALVERDE. God stay you, and stay with you all.

SOLDIERS. Amen.

Effects
cue 34
Light
cue 16

(*In the cold light there now ensues—*) Scene viii

THE MIME OF THE GREAT ASCENT.

As OLD MARTIN *describes their ordeal, the men climb the Andes. It is
a terrible progress; a stumbling, tortuous climb into the clouds, over ledges
and giant chasms, performed to an eerie, cold music made from thin whine
of huge saws—flexatons*)

OLD MARTIN. Have you ever climbed a mountain in full armour?
That's what we did, him going first the whole way up a tiny path
into the clouds, with drops sheer on both sides into nothing. For
hours we crept forward like blind men, the sweat freezing on our
faces, lugging skittery leaking horses, and pricked all the
time for the ambush that would tip us into death. Each
turn of the path it grew colder. The friendly trees of the
forest dropped away, and there were only pines.

Light
cue 17

Then they went, too, and there were just scrubby little bushes standing up in ice. All round us the rocks began to whine with cold. And
always above us, or below us, those filthy condor birds, hanging on
the air with great tasselled wings.

(*It grows darker. The music grows colder yet. The men freeze and hang
their heads for a long moment, before resuming their desperate climb*)

Then night. We lay down twos and threes together on the path and
hugged like lovers for warmth in that burning cold. And most cried.
We got up with cold iron for bones and went on. Four days like that:
groaning, not speaking; the breath like a blade in our lungs. Four
days, slowly, like flies on a wall; limping flies, dying flies, up an
endless wall of rock. A tiny army lost in the creases of the
moon.

INDIANS (*off; in a loud echo*) Ka-wai-ya!

Light
cue 18

(*The* SPANIARDS *whirl round.* VILLAC UMU *and his attendants
appear suddenly, clothed entirely in white fur. The High Priest wears a
snow-white llama head on top of his own*)

VILLAC UMU. You see Villac Umu. Chief Priest of the Sun. Why
do you come?

PIZARRO. To see the Great Inca.

VILLAC UMU. Why will you see him?

PIZARRO. To bless him.

VILLAC UMU. Why will you bless him?

PIZARRO. He is a God. I am a God.

VALVERDE (*sotto voce*) General!

PIZARRO. Be still. (*To Villac Umu*) I am a God.

VILLAC UMU. Below you is the town of Cajamarca. The great Inca orders: rest there. Tomorrow early he will come to you. Do not move from the town. Outside it is his anger—this cold which is his anger.

(VILLAC UMU *and his* ATTENDANTS *exit*)

VALVERDE. What have you done, sir?

PIZARRO. Sent him news to amaze him.

VALVERDE. I cannot approve of blasphemy.

PIZARRO. To conquer for Christ, we can surely usurp his name for a night, Father. Set on.

(*The* SPANIARDS *fan out over the stage.* DE SOTO *exits*)   **Scene ix**

OLD MARTIN. So down we went from ledge to ledge, and out on to a huge plain of eucalyptus trees, all glowing in the failing light. And there, far at the other end, lay a vast white town with roofs of straw. As night fell, we entered it. We came into an empty square, larger than any in Spain. All round it ran long white buildings, three times the height of a man. Everywhere was grave quiet. You could almost touch the silence. Up on the hill we could see the **Light** Inca's tents, and the lights from his fires ringing the **cue 19** valley.

(OLD MARTIN *exits. Some of the* SPANIARDS *sit.* ALL *look up the hillside*)

DIEGO. I wonder. How many's up there?

DE CANDIA. Ten thousand.

(DE SOTO *enters*)

DE SOTO. The town's empty. Not even a dog. Nothing.

DOMINGO. It's a trap. I know it's a trap.

PIZARRO. Felipillo! Where's that little rat? *Felipillo!*

(FELIPILLO *comes forward*)

What does this mean?

FELIPILLO. I don't know. Perhaps it is order of welcome. Great people—much honour.

VALVERDE. Nonsense, it's a trick! A brownie trick! He's got us all marked for death.

DE NIZZA. He could have killed us at any time. Why should he take such trouble with us?

PIZARRO. Because we're gods, Father. He'll change soon enough when he finds out different.

DE SOTO (*to Young Martin*) Brace up, boy! It's what you came for, isn't it? Death or glory?

YOUNG MARTIN. Sir.
PIZARRO. De Soto. De Candia.

(DE SOTO *and* DE CANDIA *go to Pizarro*)

It's got to be ambush.
DE SOTO. Round the square?
PIZARRO. Lowers the odds. Three thousand at most.
DE CANDIA. Thirty to one. Not low enough.
PIZARRO. It'll have to do. We're not fighting ten thousand or three.
One man: that's all. Get him, the rest collapse.
DE SOTO. Even if we do, they'll kill us all to get him back.
PIZARRO. If there's a knife in his throat? It's a risk. But what do
worshippers do when you snatch their God? They do nothing.
DE CANDIA. Or worship you instead.

(PIZARRO *stares at him*)

DIEGO. That's great, sir. Grab the King, grab the Kingdom!
DE NIZZA.. It would avoid bloodshed.
PIZARRO. Well—what do you say?
DE SOTO. It's the only way. It could work. With God's help.
PIZARRO. Then pray all. Disperse. Light fires. Make confession.
Battle orders at first light.

(*Most of the* SPANIARDS *disperse. Some lie down to pray and sleep.*
YOUNG MARTIN *sits apart*)

DE NIZZA (*to De Candia*) Shall I hear your confession now, my
son?
DE CANDIA. You'd best save all that for tomorrow, Father. For
the men who are left. Besides, what have we got to confess tonight
but thoughts of murder?
DE NIZZA. Then confess those, De Candia.
DE CANDIA. Why? Should I feel shame for them? What would I
say to God if I refused to destroy his enemies?
VALVERDE. More Venetian nonsense.
DE NIZZA. God has no enemies, my son. Only those nearer to him
or farther from him.
DE CANDIA. Well, my job is to aim at the far ones. I'll go and
position the guns! Excuse me.

(DE CANDIA *exits*)

PIZARRO. Diego.
DIEGO. Sir.
PIZARRO. Look to the horses. I know they're sorry, but we'll need
them brisk.
DIEGO. Yes, sir.
VALVERDE. Come, my brother, we'll pray together.

(DIEGO *and* VALVERDE *exit*)

PIZARRO. The cavalry will split and hide in the buildings, there and'there.

DE SOTO. And the infantry in file—there, and round there.

PIZARRO. Perfect. Herrada can command one flank, De Barbaran the other. Everyone hidden.   **Effects cue 35**

DE SOTO. They'll suspect them.

PIZARRO. No, the Church will greet them. Our two priests alone. Very—singular!

DE SOTO. We'll need a watchword.

PIZARRO. San Jago! Good?

DE SOTO. Good. San Jago!

(PIZARRO *comes upon* YOUNG MARTIN, *who is sitting huddled by himself*)

PIZARRO. Are you scared?

YOUNG MARTIN. No, sir—yes, sir.

PIZARRO. You're a good boy. If ever we get out of this, I'll make you a gift of whatever you ask me. Is that chivalrous enough for you?

YOUNG MARTIN. Being your page is enough, sir.

PIZARRO. Nothing else you want?

YOUNG MARTIN. A sword, sir.

PIZARRO. Ah yes, of course. Good night, Martin. Call Assembly at dawn. Battle orders!

DE SOTO. Good night, Martin. Try to sleep.

(YOUNG MARTIN *lies down to sleep. The singing of prayers is heard off, all around*)

PIZARRO. A sword's no mere bar of metal for him. His world still has sacred objects. How remote.

DIEGO. Holy Virgin, give us victory. If you do, I'll make you a present of a fine Indian cloak. But you let us down, and I'll leave you for the Virgin of the Conception, and I mean that. (*He lies down also*)   **Effects cue 36 Light cue 20**

(*The prayers die away. Silence*)

PIZARRO. This is probably our last night. If we die now, what will we have gone for?   **Scene x**

DE SOTO. Spain. Christ.

PIZARRO. I envy you, Cavalier.

DE SOTO. For what?

PIZARRO. Your service. God. King. It's all simple for you.

DE SOTO. No, sir. It's not simple. But it's what I have chosen.

PIZARRO. Yes. And what have I chosen?

DE SOTO. To be a king yourself. Or as good, if we win here.

PIZARRO. And what's that, at my age? Not only swords turn into bars of metal. Sceptres, too. What's left, De Soto?

De Soto. What you told me in Spain. A name for ballads. The man of Honour has three good lives: The Life Today. The Life to Come. The Life of Fame.

Pizarro. Fame is long. Death is longer. Does any of us ever really die for anything? Oh, I thought so once. Life was fierce with feeling. It was all hope, like on that boy. Swords shone, and armour sang, and cheese bit you, and kissing burned and death—oh well, death was going to make an exception in my case. I couldn't believe I was ever going to die. But once you know it—really *know* it—it's all over. You know you've been cheated, and nothing's the same again.

De Soto. Cheated?

Pizarro. Man, Time cheats us all the way. Children, yes—having children goes some steps to defeating it. Nothing else. It would have been good to have a son.

De Soto. Did you never think to marry?

Pizarro. With my parentage? The only sort of women who would have had me weren't the sort you married. Spain's a pile of horse dung. When I first began to think of a land out here, something in me was longing for a new place like a country after rain, washed clear of all the badges and barriers: the pebbles men drop to tell them where they are, on a plain that's got no landmarks. I used to look after women with hope, but they didn't have much time for me. One of them said—what was it?—my soul was frostbitten. There's a word for you—frostbitten. (*To Vasca*) How goes it, lad?

Vasca. A clear night, sir. Everything clear.

Pizarro (*to De Soto*) I had a girl once, on a rock by the Southern Ocean. I lay with her one afternoon in winter, wrapped up in her against the cold, and the sea-fowl screaming, and it was the best hour of my life. I felt then that sea-water, and bird-droppings, and the little pits in human flesh, were all linked together for some great end right out of the net of words to catch. Not just my words, but any-one's. Then I lost it. Time came back. For always. (*He moves away, feeling his side*)

De Soto. Does your leg still pain you?

Pizarro. Oh, yes: *that's* still fierce!

De Soto. You should try to sleep. We'll need our strength.

Pizarro. Listen, listen! Everything we feel is made of Time. All the beauties of life are shaped by it. Try to imagine a fixed sunset or the last note of a song that hung an hour, or a kiss for half of it. Try and halt a moment in our lives and it becomes maggoty at once. Even that word "moment" is wrong, because that would mean a speck of time, something you could pick up on a rag and peer at. But that's the awful trap of life. You can't escape maggots unless you go with Time. And if you go, they wriggle in you anyway.

De Soto. This is gloomy talk.

(Young Martin *moans in his sleep*)

PIZARRO. For a gloomy time. You were talking women. I loved them with all the juice in me—but oh, the cheat in *that* tenderness! What is it but a lust to own their beauty, which you never can—like trying to own the shape of a goblet by paying for it. And even if you could—if you could—it would become *you*, and grow soiled at once! I'm an old man, Cavalier. I can explain nothing. What I mean is: Time whipped up the lust in me and Time purged it. I was dandled on Time's knee and made to gurgle, then put to my sleep. I've been cheated from the moment I was born, because there's death in everything.

DE SOTO. Except in God.

PIZARRO (*after a pause*) When I was young I used to sit on the slope outside the village and watch the sun go down, and I used to think: if only I could find the place where it sinks to rest for the night, I'd find the source of life, like the beginning of a river. I used to wonder what it would be like. Perhaps an island, some strange spit of white sand, where the people never died. Never grew old, or felt pain, and never died.

DE SOTO. Sweet fancy.

PIZARRO. It's what your mind runs to when it lacks instruction. Where *does* the sun rest at night?

DE SOTO. Nowhere. It's a heavenly body sent by God to move round the earth in perpetual motion.

PIZARRO. Yes. You know this?

DE SOTO. All Europe knows it.

PIZARRO. What if they were wrong? What if it settled here each evening, somewhere in those great mountains like a God laid down to sleep? To a savage mind it must make a fine God. I myself can't fix anything nearer to a thought of worship than standing at dawn and watching it fill the world. Like the coming of something eternal against going flesh. What a fantastic wonder that any man on earth should dare to say: 'That's my father. My father: the sun'! It's silly—but tremendous. You know—strange nonsense: ever since I first heard of him I've dreamed of him every night. A black king with blazing eyes, sporting the sun for a crown. Tell me what that means.

DE SOTO. I've no skill with dreams. Perhaps a soothsayer would tell you: 'The Inca's your enemy. You dream his emblem to increase your hate.'

PIZARRO. But I feel no enemy.

DE SOTO. Surely you do.

PIZARRO. No. None. Only that of all meetings I have made in my life, this with him is the one I have to make. Maybe it's my death. Or maybe new life. I feel just this: all my days have been a path to this one morning.   **Light cue 21**.

(OLD MARTIN *enters*)

OLD MARTIN. The sixteenth of November, fifteen hundred and thirty-two.

YOUNG MARTIN (*rising*) First light, sir.
DE NIZZA (*off; singing*) Exsurge Domine.

SOLDIERS (*singing in unison*) Exsurge Domine.
PIZARRO. Ha ha!
DE SOTO. Why do you laugh now?
PIZARRO. That's a mystery. And not much, either,

(*All the* COMPANY *enter, chanting*)

DE NIZZA. Deus meus eripe me de manu peccatoris.
SOLDIERS. Deus meus eripe me de manu peccatoris.

(ALL *kneel, spread across the stage*)

VALVERDE. Many strong bulls have compassed me.
DE NIZZA. They have gaped upon me with their mouths, as a lion ravening.
VALVERDE. I am poured out like water, and all my bones are scattered.
DE NIZZA. My heart is like wax, melting in the midst of my bowels. My tongue cleaves to my jaws, and thou hast brought me into the dust of death.

(ALL *freeze*)

OLD MARTIN. The dust of death. It was in our noses. The full scare came to us quickly, like plague.

(ALL *heads turn*)

The men were crammed in buildings all round the square.

(ALL *stand*)

They stood there shivering, making water where they stood. An hour went by. Two. Three.

(ALL *remain absolutely still*)

Five. Not a move from the Indian camp. Not a sound from ours. Only the weight of the day. A hundred and sixty men in full armour, cavalry mounted, infantry at the ready, standing in dead silence—glued in a trance of waiting.
PIZARRO. Hold fast now. Come on—you're gods. Hold stiff. Don't even blink your eyes, that's too much noise.
OLD MARTIN. Seven.
PIZARRO. Stiff. Stiff. You're your own masters, boys! Not peasant any more. This is your time. You've chosen it—own it. Live it.
OLD MARTIN. Nine. Ten hours passed. There were few of us then who didn't feel the cold begin to crawl.

PIZARRO (*whispering*) Send him, send him, send him, send him.

OLD MARTIN. Dread comes with the evening air. Even the priest's arm fails.

PIZARRO. The sun's going out!

OLD MARTIN. No one looks at his neighbour. Then, with the shadow of night slithering towards us . . .

YOUNG MARTIN. *They're coming, sir!* Down the hill!

DE SOTO. How many?

YOUNG MARTIN. Hundreds, sir!

DE CANDIA. Thousands—two or three!

PIZARRO. Can you see *him*?

DE CANDIA. No, not yet.

DOMINGO. What's that? Out there in front—they're doing something.

VASCA. Looks like sweeping. They're sweeping the road.

DIEGO. Saving Jesus! They're sweeping the road!

DOMINGO. For *him*! They're sweeping the road for him! Five hundred of 'em sweeping the road!

SALINAS. Christ in Heaven!

PIZARRO. Are they armed?

DE CANDIA. To the teeth.

DE SOTO. How?

DE CANDIA. Axes and spears.

YOUNG MARTIN. Everything's glittering, glittering red.

DIEGO. It's the sun! Like someone's cut it.

VASCA. Squirting blood all over the sky.

DOMINGO. It's an omen!

SALINAS. Shut up.

DOMINGO. It must be. Look for yourself. The whole country's bleeding. It's an omen!

VALVERDE. This is the day foretold by the Angel of the Apocalypse. Satan reigns on the altars, jeering at the true God.

DOMINGO. Oh God! My God! Oh God! My God! Oh God! My God!

VALVERDE. The earth teems with corrupt kings.

DE SOTO (*to Domingo*) Control yourself!

DE CANDIA. They've stopped.

YOUNG MARTIN. They're throwing things down, sir!

PIZARRO. Things?

DE CANDIA. Weapons.

PIZARRO. No!

DIEGO. Yes, sir. I can see. All their weapons. They're dropping them in a pile. A great pile!

VASCA. They're laying down their arms.

SALINAS. I don't believe it!

VASCA. They are. They are leaving everything.

DOMINGO. It's a miracle.

DE SOTO. Why? *Why?*

PIZARRO. Because we're gods. You see? You don't approach gods with weapons.

Effects
cue 38
Light
cue 23

(*Strange music is heard faintly in the distance. Through all the ensuing it grows louder and louder*)

DE SOTO. What's that?

YOUNG MARTIN. It's him, sir—he's coming.

DIEGO. Oh, *look*! Christ Almighty, I don't believe it—it's not happening . . . !

DE SOTO. Steady, man.

PIZARRO. Come on then. Come on! Come on!

DE SOTO. General, it's time to hide.

PIZARRO. Yes, quick! No one man must be seen but the priests. Out there, Fathers! Felipillo, stand between them!

DE SOTO. Come on—jump to it, men!

(*Only now do the* SOLDIERS *break, scatter and vanish.* VALVERDE *and* DE NIZZA *take up positions with* FELIPILLO)

PIZARRO (*to Young Martin*) You, too.

YOUNG MARTIN. Till the fighting?

PIZARRO. All the time for you, fighting or no. Take him, De Soto!

DE SOTO. Save you, General.

PIZARRO. And you, San Jago!

DE SOTO. San Jago! Come on!

(DE SOTO *exits with Young Martin*)

DE CANDIA. There are seven gunners on the roof. And three over there.

PIZARRO. Watch the cross-fire.

DE CANDIA. I'll wait for your signal.

PIZARRO. Then sound yours.

DE CANDIA. You'll hear it.

(DE CANDIA *exits*)

PIZARRO. Now . . . NOW! NOW!!

Effects
cue 39
Light
cue 24

(PIZARRO *hurries off, leaving the* PRIESTS *and* FELIPILLO *alone, with* OLD MARTIN *standing apart.*

Scene xii

The music crashes over the stage as the INDIAN *procession enters in an astonishing explosion of colour. The King's* ATTENDANTS—*many of them playing musical instruments: reed pipes, cymbals and giant maraccas—are as gay as parrots. They wear costumes of orange and yellow, and fantastic head-dresses of gold and feathers, with eyes embossed on them in staring black enamel. By contrast* ATAHUALLPA INCA *presents a picture of utter simplicity. He is dressed from head to foot in white: across his eyes is a mask of jade mosaic, and round his head a circlet of plain gold. Silence falls.* ATAHUALLPA *glares about him*)

ATAHUALLPA (*haughtily*) Where is the God?
VALVERDE. I am a priest of God.
ATAHUALLPA (*through Felipillo*) I do not want the
priest. I want the God. Where is he? He sent me greeting.
VALVERDE. That was our General. Our God cannot be seen.
ATAHUALLPA. *I* may see him.
VALVERDE. No. He was killed by men and went into the sky.
ATAHUALLPA. A god cannot be killed. See my father. You cannot
kill him. He lives for ever and looks over his children every day.
VALVERDE. I am the answer to all mysteries. Hark, pagan, and I
will expound.
OLD MARTIN. And so he did, from the Creation to our Lord's
ascension.

   (OLD MARTIN *exits*)

VALVERDE (*walking among the Indians* R) And when he went he left
the Pope as Regent for him.
DE NIZZA (*walking among the Indians* L) And when he went he left
the Pope as Regent for him.
VALVERDE. He has commanded our King to bring all men to
belief in the true God.
DE NIZZA. He has commanded our King to bring all men to
belief in the true God.
VALVERDE⎱ (*together*) ⎰In Christ's name therefore I charge
DE NIZZA ⎰   ⎱you: yield yourself his willing vassal.
ATAHUALLPA. I am the vassal of no man.
INDIANS (*falling flat*) Ka-wai-ya!
ATAHUALLPA. I am the greatest Prince on earth. Your King is
great. He has sent you far across the water. So he is my brother. But
your Pope is mad. He gives away countries that are not his. His
faith is also mad.
VALVERDE. Beware!
ATAHUALLPA. Ware you! You kill my people; you make them
slaves. By what power?
VALVERDE. By this. (*He offers a Bible through Felipillo*) The Word
of God.

   (ATAHUALLPA *holds the Bible to his ear. He listens intently. He shakes
   it*)

ATAHUALLPA. No word. (*He smells the book, and then licks it.
Finally he throws it down impatiently*) God is angry with your insults.
VALVERDE. Blasphemy!
ATAHUALLPA. God is angry! *Angry!*
VALVERDE. Francisco Pizarro, do you stay your hand when Christ
is insulted? Let this pagan feel the power of your arm.
I absolve you all! San Jago!

   (PIZARRO *appears above with sword drawn, and in
   a great voice sings out his battle cry*)

PIZARRO. SAN JAGO Y CIERRA ESPANA!

(*Instantly all the* SOLDIERS *rush on from every side, echoing the great cry*)

SOLDIERS. *SAN JAGO!*   **Effects
                               cue 41**

There is a tense pause. The INDIANS *look at this ring of armed men in terror. A violent drumming begins and there ensues—*

THE MIME OF THE GREAT MASSACRE

To a savage music, wave upon wave of INDIANS *are slaughtered and rise again to protect their lord, who stands bewildered in their midst. It is all in vain. Relentlessly the* SPANISH SOLDIERS *hew their way through the ranks of feathered attendants towards their quarry. They surround him.* SALINAS *snatches the crown off his head and tosses it up to* PIZARRO, *who catches it and to a great shout crowns himself. All the* INDIANS *cry out in horror.*

The drum hammers on relentlessly while ATAHUALLPA *is led off at swordpoint by the whole band of* SPANIARDS. *At the same time, dragged from the middle of the sun by howling* INDIANS, *a vast bloodstained cloth bellies out over the stage. ALL rush off; their screams fill the theatre. The* LIGHTS *fade out slowly on the rippling cloth of blood.*   **Light
                                                            cue 26**

ACT II

THE KILL

Scene i

SCENE—*The same.*
Darkness. A bitter Inca Lament is intoned. The LIGHTS *come up a little. The bloodstained cloth still lies over the stage. In the sun chamber* ATAHUALLPA *stands in chains, his back to the audience, his white robe dirty with blood and his black hair hanging down it like a mane. Although he is unmasked we cannot yet see his face. Below,* OLD MARTIN *appears. From the opposite side* YOUNG MARTIN *enters, stumbling with shock.*

Effects
cue 42
Light
cue 27

Light
cue 28

OLD MARTIN. Look at the warrior where he stands. Glory on his sword. Salvation in his new spurs. One of the knights at last. The very perfect knight, Sir Martin, Sir Eager, tender in virtue, body-guard of Christ. Jesus, we are all eased out of kids' dreams: but who can be *ripped* out of them and live loving after? Three thousand Indians were killed in that square. The only Spaniard to be wounded was the General, scratched by a sword whilst protecting his Royal prisoner. That night, as I knelt vomiting into a canal, the empire of the Incas stopped. The spring of the clock was snapped. For a thousand miles men sat down, not knowing what to do.

(DE SOTO *enters*)

Effects
cue 43

DE SOTO (*to Young Martin*) Well, boy, what is it? They weren't armed, is that it? If they had been we would be dead now.

YOUNG MARTIN. Honourably dead! Not alive and shamed.

DE SOTO. And Christ would be dead here, too, scarcely born. When I first breathed blood, it was in my lungs for days. But the time comes when you won't even sniff when it pours over your feet. See, boy, here and now it's kill or get killed. And if we go, we betray Christ, whose coming we are here to make.

YOUNG MARTIN. You talk as if we're porters, sent to shove open the door for him.

DE SOTO. So we are. That's our part.

YOUNG MARTIN. No! He's with us now—at all times—or never.

DE SOTO. He's with *us*, yes, but not with *them*. After he is, there will be time for mercy. Do you see?

YOUNG MARTIN. When there is no danger! Some mercy!

DE SOTO. Would you put Christ in danger, then?

YOUNG MARTIN. He can look after himself.

DE SOTO. He can't. That's why he needs servants.

YOUNG MARTIN. To kill for him?

DE SOTO. If necessary. And it was here. My parish priest used to say: 'There must always be dying to make new life.' I think of that whenever I draw the sword. My constant thought is: I must be Winter for our Lord to be Spring. Ice may be thawed with blood.

YOUNG MARTIN. I don't understand. I don't understand anything.

(PIZARRO *and* FELIPILLO *enter*)

PIZARRO. Stand up when the Second addresses you. What are you, a defiled girl? (*To De Soto*) I've sent De Candia back to the Garrison. Reinforcements should be there presently. Come now: let's meet this King.

Light
cue 29

(PIZARRO, FELIPILLO *and* DE SOTO *move upstage and bow. Above*, OELLO *and* INTI COUSSI *enter and kneel on either side of Atahuallpa.* ATAHUALLPA *ignores the Embassy below*)

Scene ii

My lord, I am Francisco Pizarro, General of Spain. It is an honour to speak with you. (*He pauses*) You are very tall, my lord. In my country are no such tall men. (*He pauses*) My lord, won't you speak?

(ATAHUALLPA *turns. For the first time we see his face, carved in a mould of fierce arrogance. His whole bearing displays the most entire dignity and natural grace. When he moves or speaks it is always with the consciousness of his divine origin, his sacred function, and his absolute power*)

ATAHUALLPA (*to Felipillo*) Tell him I am Atahuallpa Capac. Son of the Sun, Son of the Moon, Lord of the Four Quarters. Why does he not kneel?

FELIPILLO. The Inca says he wishes he had killed you when you first came.

PIZARRO. Why didn't he?

ATAHUALLPA. He lied to me. He is not a god. I came for blessing. He sharpened his knives on the shoulders of my servants. I have no word for *him* whose word is evil!

FELIPILLO. He says he wants to make slaves of your best warriors, then kill all the others. Especially *you* he would kill, because you are old: no use as slave.

PIZARRO. Tell him he will live to rue those intentions.

FELIPILLO. You make my master angry. He will kill you to-morrow. Then he will give that wife Oello to me for my pleasure.

ATAHUALLPA. Do you speak this before my eyes?

YOUNG MARTIN. General.

PIZARRO. What?

YOUNG MARTIN. Excuse me, sir, but I don't think you're being translated aright.

PIZARRO. You don't?

YOUNG MARTIN. No, sir. Nor the King to you. I know a little of the language and he said nothing about slaves.

PIZARRO. You! What are you saying?

FELIPILLO. General lord. This boy know nothing how to speak. A boy. A poor boy . . .!

YOUNG MARTIN. I know more than you think. I know you're lying. He's after the woman, General. I saw him before, in the square, grabbing at her.

PIZARRO. It that true?

YOUNG MARTIN. As I live, sir.

PIZARRO. What do you say?

FELIPILLO. General lord, I speak wonderful for you. No one speak so wonderful.

PIZARRO. What about that girl?

FELIPILLO. You give her as present to me, yes?

PIZARRO. The Inca's wife?

FELIPILLO. Inca has many wives. This one, small, not famous.

PIZARRO. Get out!

FELIPILLO. General lord!

PIZARRO. You work another trick like this and I'll swear I'll hang you. Out!

(FELIPILLO *spits at Pizarro and runs out*)

Could you take his place?

YOUNG MARTIN. With work, sir.

PIZARRO. Work, then. It's vital! Come, make a start. Ask him his age.

YOUNG MARTIN (*to Atahuallpa*) My lord, how old are him? I mean 'you' . . .?

ATAHUALLPA. I have been on earth thirty and three years. What age is your master?

YOUNG MARTIN. Sixty-three.

ATAHUALLPA. All those years have taught him nothing but wickedness.

YOUNG MARTIN. That's not true.

PIZARRO. What does he say?

YOUNG MARTIN. I don't quite understand, my lord . . .

(YOUNG MARTIN *exits*)

OLD MARTIN. So it was I became the general's interpreter and was privy to everything that passed between them during the next terrible months. The Inca tongue was very hard, but to please my adored master I worked at it for hours, and with each passing day found out more of it.

(PIZARRO *exits, followed by* DE SOTO. OELLO *and*   **Light**
INTI COUSSI *exit*   **cue 30**

YOUNG MARTIN *enters above, with a pack of cards.* OLD
MARTIN *watches from below for a moment, then exits*)   **Scene iii**

YOUNG MARTIN. Good day, my lord. I have a game here to
amuse you. No Spaniard is complete without them. I take half and
you take half. Then we fight. These are Churchmen with their
pyxes. The Nobility with their swords. The Merchants with the
gold, and the Poor with their sticks.
ATAHUALLPA. What are the poor?
YOUNG MARTIN. Those who've got no gold. They suffer for this.
ATAHUALLPA. *Aiyah!*
YOUNG MARTIN. What are you thinking, my lord?   **Light**
ATAHUALLPA. That my people will suffer.   **cue 31**

(PIZARRO *and* DE SOTO *enter below*)

PIZARRO (*briskly*) Good day, my lord. How are you this morning?
ATAHUALLPA. You want gold. That is why you came here.
PIZARRO. My lord . . .
ATAHUALLPA. You cannot hide from me. (*Showing Pizarro the
card of the Poor*) You want gold. I know. Speak.
PIZARRO (*carefully*) You have gold?
ATAHUALLPA. It is the sweat of the sun. It belongs to me.
PIZARRO. Is there much?
ATAHUALLPA. Make me free, I would fill this room.
PIZARRO. Fill?
DE SOTO. It's not possible.
ATAHUALLPA. I am Atahuallpa and I say it.
PIZARRO. How long?
ATAHUALLPA. Two showings of my mother moon. But it will not
be done.
PIZARRO. Why not?
ATAHUALLPA. You must swear to free me and you have no swear
to give.
PIZARRO. You wrong me, my lord.
ATAHUALLPA. No, it is in your face, no swear.
PIZARRO. I never broke my word with you. I never promised you
safety. If once I did, you would have it.
ATAHUALLPA. Do you now?
DE SOTO. Refuse, sir. You could never free him.
PIZARRO. It won't come to that.
DE SOTO. It could.
PIZARRO. Never. Can you think how much gold it would take?
Even half would drown us in riches!
DE SOTO. General, you can only give your word where you can
keep it.
PIZARRO. I'll never have to break it. It's the same case.
DE SOTO. It's not. Sir, it's not.
PIZARRO. Oh, God's bread, your niceties! He's offering more than

any conqueror has ever seen. Alexander, Tamburlaine, or who you please. I mean to have it.

De Soto. So. At your age gold is no loadstone! As you said!

Pizarro. Nor more it is. I promised my men gold. Yes? He stands between them and that gold. If I don't make this bargain now, he'll die; the men will demand it.

De Soto. And what's that to you if he does?

Pizarro. *I want him alive!* At least for a while.

De Soto. You're thinking of how you dreamed him.

Pizarro. He has some meaning for me, this man-God. An immortal man in whom all his people live completely. He has an answer for time. An answer . . .

De Soto. If it was true.

Pizarro. Yes, if . . .

De Soto. General, be careful. I don't understand you in full, but I know this: what you do now can never be undone.

Pizarro. Words, my dear Cavalier. They don't touch me. This way I'll have gold for my men and him there safe. That's enough for the moment. (*To Atahuallpa*) Now, you must keep the peace meanwhile, not strive to escape, nor urge your men to help you. So, swear.

Atahuallpa. I swear!

Pizarro. Then I swear, too. Soldier to soldier. Pig-herd to King! Fill that room with gold and I will set you free.

De Soto. General . . .

Pizarro (*furiously*) Oh, come, man! He never will.

De Soto. I think this man performs what he swears. Pray God we won't pay bitterly for this.

(De Soto *marches off.* Old Martin *enters*)

Pizarro. My lord . . .

(Atahuallpa *ignores Pizarro*)

(*To Young Martin*) Well spoken, lad. Your services increase every day.

Young Martin. Thank you, sir.

(Pizarro *exits.* Young Martin *leaves* Atahuallpa *alone in the Sun Chamber*)

Old Martin. The room was twenty-two feet long by seventeen wide. The mark on the wall was nine feet high.

Atahuallpa. ATAHUALLPA SPEAKS! Atahuallpa needs! Atahuallpa commands! Bring him gold. From the palaces. From the temples. From all buildings in the great places. From walls of pleasure and roofs of omen. From floors of feasting and ceilings of death. Bring him the gold of Quito and Pachamacac! Bring him the gold of Cuzco and Coricancha! Bring him the gold of Vilcanota! Bring him the gold of

Light
cue 32
Effects
cue 44

Colae! Of Amaraes and Arequipa. (*Howling*) Bring him the gold of
the Chimu! Put up a mountain of gold, and free your
sun from his prison of clouds!   **Effects**
   OLD MARTIN. It was agreed that the gold collected   **cue 45**
was not to be melted beforehand into bars, so that the   **Light**
Inca got the benefit of the space between them. Then he   **cue 33**
was moved out of his prison to make way for the trea-   **Light**
sure, and given more comfortable state.   **cue 34**

   (ATAHUALLPA *leaves the Sun Chamber.*
   Slowly the great cloth of blood is dragged off by two   **Scene iv**
INDIANS *as* ATAHUALLPA *appears. He advances to the*
middle of the stage. He claps his hands, once. Immediately a   **Effects**
gentle hum is heard and INDIANS *appear with new clothing.*   **cue 46**
From their wrists hang tiny golden cymbals and small bells;
to the soft clash and tinkle of these little instruments, his servants remove the
Inca's bloodstained garments and put on him clean ones)

He was allowed to see his wives and audience his nobles. The little
loads they bore were a sign of reverence.

   (VILLAC UMU *and* CHALLCUCHIMO *enter*)

He was dressed in his royal cloak, made from the skins of vampire
birds, and his ears were hung again with the weight of noble
responsibility.

   (ATAHUALLPA *is cloaked, a collar of turquoises is placed round his*
neck and heavy gold rings are placed on his ears. While this is happening
there is a fresh tinkling, and more INDIANS *enter, carrying his meal in*
musical dishes—plates like tambourines from whose rims hang bells, or in
whose lower shelves are tiny golden balls. OELLO *and* INTI COUSSI *enter*
with the others. The stage is filled with chimes and delicate clatter, and
above it the perpetual humming of masked servants)

His meals were served as they always had been. I remember his
favourite food was a stewed lamb, garnished with
sweet potatoes.   **Light**
                                                                 cue 35
   (*The food is served to Atahuallpa in this manner:* OELLO
takes meat out of a bowl, places it in her hands. ATAHUAL-
LPA *lowers his face to it, while* OELLO *turns her own face from him out of*
respect)

What he didn't eat was burnt, and if he spilled any on himself, his
clothes were burnt also.

   (OELLO *rises and quietly removes the dish.* FELIPILLO   **Effects**
rushes on and knocks it violently from her hand.   **cue 47**

   FELIPILLO. You're going to burn it? Why? Because
your husband is God? How stupid! Stupid, stupid!

(FELIPILLO *grabs Oello and flings her to the ground*)

INDIANS (*crying out in horror*) Ka-wai-ya!

FELIPILLO (*to Atahuallpa*) Yes, I touch her! Make me dead! You are a god. Make me dead with your eyes!

VILLAC UMU. What you have said kills you. You will be buried in the earth alive.

(*There is a pause. For a moment* FELIPILLO *half believes this. Then he laughs and kisses Oello on the throat. As she screams and struggles* YOUNG MARTIN *rushes in*)

YOUNG MARTIN. Felipillo, stop it!

(VALVERDE *hurries in from the opposite side, followed by* DE NIZZA)

VALVERDE. Felipillo! Is it for this we saved you from Hell? Your old God encouraged lust. Your new God will damn you for it. Leave him! Now.

(FELIPILLO *runs off*)

(*To the Indians*) Go—all of you!

(*There is a pause. No one moves.* ATAHUALLPA *claps his hands twice. All the* SERVANTS *bow and exit*)

(*To Atahuallpa*) Now, my lord, let us take up our talk again. Tell me—I am but a simple priest—as an undoubted God, do you live for ever here on earth?

VILLAC UMU. Here on earth gods come one after another, young and young again, to protect the people of the Sun. Then they go up to his great place in the sky, at his will.

VALVERDE. What if they are killed in battle?

VILLAC UMU. If it is not the Sun's time for them to go, he will return them to life again in the next day's light.

VALVERDE. How comforting. And has any Inca so returned?

VILLAC UMU. No.

VALVERDE. Curious.

VILLAC UMU. This means only that all Incas have died in the Sun's time.

VALVERDE. Clever.

VILLAC UMU. No. True.

VALVERDE. Tell me this, how can the Sun have a child?

VILLAC UMU. How can your God have a child, since you say he has no body?

VALVERDE. He is spirit—inside us.

VILLAC UMU. Your God is inside you? How can this be?

ATAHUALLPA. They eat him. First he becomes a biscuit, and then they eat him. (*He bares his teeth and laughs soundlessly*) I have seen this. At praying they say: 'This is the body of our God.' Then they drink his blood. It is very bad. Here in my empire we do not eat men. My family forbade it many years past.

VALVERDE. You are being deliberately stupid.

VILLAC UMU. Why do you eat God? Is it to have his strength?

DE NIZZA. Yes, my lord.

VILLAC UMU. But your God is weak. He fights with no man. That is why he was killed.

DE NIZZA. He *wanted* to be killed, so he could share death with us.

ATAHUALLPA. *So* he needed killers to help him, though you say killing is bad.

VALVERDE. This is the devil's tongue.

DE NIZZA. My lord must see that when God becomes man he can no longer act perfectly.

ATAHUALLPA. Why?

DE NIZZA. He joins us in our state of sin.

ATAHUALLPA. Speak out—'sin'.

DE NIZZA. Let me picture it to you as a prison cell, the bars made of our imperfections. Through them we glimpse a fair country where it is always morning. We wish we could walk there, or else forget the place entirely. But we cannot snap the bars, or if we do others grow in their stead.

ATAHUALLPA. All your pictures are of prisons and chains.

DE NIZZA. All life is of chains. We are chained to food, and fire in the winter. To innocence lost, but its memory unlost. And to needing each other.

ATAHUALLPA. I need no one.

DE NIZZA. That is not true.

ATAHUALLPA. I am the Sun. I need only the sky.

DE NIZZA. That is not true, Atahuallpa. The sun is a ball of fire. Nothing more.

ATAHUALLPA. How?

DE NIZZA. Nothing more.

(*With terrible speed,* ATAHUALLPA *rises to strike De Nizza*)

VALVERDE. Down! Do you dare lift your hand against a priest? Sit!

(ATAHUALLPA *does not move*)

DE NIZZA. You do not feel your people, my lord, because you do not love them.

ATAHUALLPA. Speak out—'love'.

DE NIZZA. It is not known in your kingdom. At home we can say to our ladies: 'I love you', or to our native earth. It means we rejoice in their lives. But a man cannot say this to the woman he *must* marry at twenty-five; or to the strip of land allotted to him at birth which he must till till he dies. Love must be free, or else it alters away. Command it to your court; it will send a deputy. Let God

order ít to fill our hearts, it becomes useless to him. It is stronger
than iron; yet in a fist of force it melts. It is a coin that sparkles in
the hand, yet in the pocket it goes to rust. Love is the only door from
the prison of ourselves. It is the eagerness of God to enter that
prison, to take on pain, and imagine lust, so that the torn soldier,
or the spent lecher, can call out in his defeat: 'You know
this, too, so help me from it.'

Effects
cue 48

(*A further music of bells and humming is heard.* OLD
MARTIN *enters, and speaks during the following.*

Light
cue 36

THE FIRST GOLD PROCESSION

Guarded closely by Spanish SOLDIERS, *a line of* INDIAN PORTERS
*enters, each carrying a stylized gold object—utensils and ornaments.
They cross the stage and exit. Almost simultaneously, above, similar
objects are hung up by the* INDIANS *in the middle of the Sun*)

OLD MARTIN (*during the above*) The first gold arrived. Much of it
was in big plates weighing up to seventy-five pounds, the rest in
objects of amazing skill. Knives of ceremony; lacy collars and
fretted crowns; funeral gloves; and red-stained death masks, gog-
gling at us with profound, enamel eyes. Some days there were things
worth thirty or forty gold pesos—but we weren't satis-
fied with that.

Light
cue 37

(OLD MARTIN *exits.* PIZARRO, YOUNG MARTIN, *and* DE SOTO
enter)

PIZARRO. I find you wanting in honesty. A month has passed: the
room isn't a quarter full.

ATAHUALLPA. My kingdom is great—porters are slow. You will
see more gold before long.

PIZARRO. The rumour is we'll see a rising before long.

ATAHUALLPA. Not a leaf stirs in my kingdom without my leave.
If you do not trust me, send to Cuzco, my capital. See how quiet my
people sit.

PIZARRO. Good. I will. De Soto, you leave immediately with a
force of thirty.

CHALLCUCHIMA. God is tied by his word, like you. But if he raised
one nail of one finger of one hand, you would all die that same
raising.

PIZARRO. So be it. You play us false, both these shall die before us.

ATAHUALLPA (*remotely*) There are many priests, many generals.
These can die.

VALVERDE. Mother of God! There's no conversion possible for
this man.

DE SOTO. You cannot say that, sir.

VALVERDE. Satan has many forms and there sits one! As for his advisers, it is *you*, Priest, who stiffens him against me. You, General, who whisper revolt.

CHALLCUCHIMA. You lie. God does not need my whisper!

VALVERDE. Leave him!

(*As before, no one moves until* ATAHUALLPA *has clapped his hands twice. Then, immediately,* VILLAC UMU *and* CHALLCUCHIMA *bow and leave*)

Pagan filth!

DE SOTO. I'll go and make inspection. Good-bye, my lord, we'll meet in a month. General.

(DE SOTO *exits*)

VALVERDE. Beware Pizarro. Give him the slack, he will destroy us all.

(VALVERDE *exits*)

DE NIZZA. The Father has great zeal.

PIZARRO. Oh yes, great zeal to see the devil in a poor dark man.

DE NIZZA. Not so poor, General. A man who is the soul of his kingdom. Look hard, you *will* find Satan here, because here is a country which denies the right to hunger.

PIZARRO. You call hunger a right?

DE NIZZA. Of course. It gives life meaning. Look around you: happiness has no feel for men here, since they are forbidden unhappiness. They hold everything in common. So they have nothing to give one another. They are part of the seasons, no more; as indistinguishable as mules, as predictable as trees. All men are born unequal: this is a divine gift. And want is their birthright. Where you deny this and there is no hope of any new love: where tomorrow is abolished, and no man ever thinks: 'I can change myself', there you have the rule of Antichrist. Atahuallpa, I will not rest until I have brought you to the true God.

ATAHUALLPA (*springing up*) No! He is not true! Where is he? Where? *There* is my father—Sun! You see now only by his wish! Yet try to see into him and he will darken your eyes for ever! With hot burning he pulls up the corn, and we feed. With cold burning he shrinks it, and we starve. These are his burnings and our life. Do not speak to me again of your God. He is nowhere!

(ATAHUALLPA *turns his back on De Nizza.* PIZARRO *laughs.* DE NIZZA *exits hurriedly*)

PIZARRO. You said you'd hear the Holy Men.   **Scene v**

ATAHUALLPA. They are fools.

PIZARRO. They are not fools.

ATAHUALLPA. Do you believe them?

PIZARRO. For certain.

ATAHUALLPA. Look into me. You do not believe them.

PIZARRO. You dare not say that to me . . .

ATAHUALLPA. You do not believe them. Their God is   **Effects**
not in your face.   **cue 49**

(PIZARRO *retreats from* ATAHUALLPA, *who begins to sing in a strange voice*)

> You must not rob, O little finch.
> The harvest maize, O little finch.
> The trap is set, O little finch.
> To catch you quick, O little finch.
>
> Ask that black bird, O little finch.
> Nailed on a branch, O little finch.
> Where are her plumes, O little finch.
> Where is her heart, O little finch.
>
> She is cut up, O little finch.
> For stealing grain, O little finch.
> See, see the fate, O little finch.
> Of robber birds, O little finch.

This is a harvest song. For you.

PIZARRO. For me?

ATAHUALLPA. Yes.

PIZARRO. Robber birds.

ATAHUALLPA. Yes.

PIZARRO. You are a robber bird yourself.

ATAHUALLPA. Explain this.

PIZARRO. You killed your brother to get the throne.

ATAHUALLPA. He was a fool. His body was a man. His head was a child.

PIZARRO. But he was the rightful king.

ATAHUALLPA. I was the rightful God! My Sky Father shouted: 'Rise up! In you lives your Earth Father, Huayana the Warrior. Your brother is fit only to tend herds, but you were born to tend my people.' So I killed him, and the land smiled.

PIZARRO. That was my work long ago. Tending herds.

ATAHUALLPA. It was not your work. You are a warrior. It is in your face.

PIZARRO. You see much of my face.

ATAHUALLPA. I see my father.

PIZARRO. You do me honour, lad.

ATAHUALLPA. Speak true. If in your home your brother was King, but fit only for herds, would you take his crown?

PIZARRO. If I could.

ATAHUALLPA. And then you would kill him.

PIZARRO. No.

ATAHUALLPA. If you could not keep it for fear of his friends, unless he was dead, you would kill him.

PIZARRO. Let me give you another case. If I come to a country and seize a king's crown, but for fear of his friends cannot keep it unless I kill him, what do I do?

ATAHUALLPA. So.

PIZARRO. So.

(ATAHUALLPA *moves away, offended*)

Oh come, it is only a game we play. Tell me—did you hate your brother?

ATAHUALLPA. No. He was ugly like a llama, like his mother. *My* mother was beautiful.

PIZARRO. I did not know my mother. She was not my father's wife. She left me at the church door for anyone to find. There's talk still in the village, how I was suckled by a sow.

ATAHUALLPA. You are not then . . .?

PIZARRO. Legitimate? No, my lord. No more than you.

ATAHUALLPA. So.

PIZARRO. So.

ATAHUALLPA (*after a pause*) To be born so is a sign for a great man.

PIZARRO (*smiling*) I think so, too.

(ATAHUALLPA *removes one of his golden ear-rings and hangs it on Pizarro's ear*)

And what is that?

ATAHUALLPA. This is the mark of a great man. Only the most important men may wear them. The ones nearest to me.

YOUNG MARTIN. Very becoming, my lord. Look, sir.

(YOUNG MARTIN *hands Pizarro a dagger*. PIZARRO *looks at himself in the blade*)

PIZARRO. I have never seemed so distinguished to myself. (*To Atahuallpa*) I thank you.

ATAHUALLPA. Now you must learn the dance of the aylu.

YOUNG MARTIN. The dance of a nobleman, sir.

ATAHUALLPA. Only he can do this. I will show you.

(PIZARRO *sits*. ATAHUALLPA *dances a ferocious mime of a warrior killing his foes. It is very difficult to execute, demanding great litheness and physical stamina. As suddenly as it began, it is over*)

You dance.

PIZARRO. I can't dance, lad.

ATAHUALLPA (*sternly*) You are my noble now. *Dance!*

PIZARRO. I'm not built for dancing.

ATAHUALLPA. You are my noble now—dance!

(ATAHUALLPA *sits to watch. Seeing there is no help for it,* PIZARRO

rises and clumsily tries to copy the dance. The effect is so grotesque that
YOUNG MARTIN *cannot help laughing.* PIZARRO *lunges, slips, slides, and
finally starts to laugh himself. He gives up the attempt)*

PIZARRO (*to* Atahuallpa) You make me laugh! (*In*   Light
sudden wonder) You make me laugh!   cue 38

(ATAHUALLPA *consults* YOUNG MARTIN, *who explains.* ATAHUALLPA
nods gravely. Tentatively, PIZARRO *extends his hand to Atahuallpa. As
tentatively, because he has never been touched before,* ATAHUALLPA *takes
it and rises. Quietly,* PIZARRO *and* ATAHUALLPA *exit together upstage.*
YOUNG MARTIN *follows.* OLD MARTIN *enters from another direction)*

OLD MARTIN. Slowly the pile increased. The army   Scene vi
waited nervously and licked its lips. Greed began to rise   Effects
in us like a tide of sea.   cue 50

(*The music of bells and humming begins.*

THE SECOND GOLD PROCESSION AND
THE RAPE OF THE SUN

A line of INDIAN PORTERS *enters, bearing gold objects. Like the first,
this instalment of treasure is guarded by Spanish soldiers, but they are less
disciplined now.* DOMINGO *enters with a necklace.* RODAS *tries to snatch
it. They clash swords briefly. The music chatters.*

Above in the chamber, the treasure is piled up as before. DIEGO *and the*
CHAVEZ BROTHERS *are seen supervising. They begin to explore the Sun
itself, leaning out of the chamber and prodding at the petals with their
halberds. Suddenly* DIEGO *gives a cry of triumph, drives his halberd into
a slot in one of the rays and pulls out the gold inlay. The sun gives a deep
groan like the sound of a great animal being wounded)*

DIEGO. Salinas, look!

(*The* SOLDIERS *rush up to the chamber imitating Inca chants, and tear
off the petals. Great groans fill the air. In a moment only the great gold
frame remains: a broken blackened sun.* DE SOTO *enters)*

Welcome back, sir.   Light
DE SOTO. Diego, thank you.   cue 39
DIEGO. What's it like, sir? Is there trouble?
DE SOTO. Grave quiet. Terrible. Men just standing in fields for
hundreds of miles. Waiting for their God to come back to them.

(*During the following a line of* INDIANS, *bent double, is loaded with
the torn-off petals from the sun)*

DIEGO. Well, if he does they'll be fighters again and we're for the
lime-pit.
DE SOTO. How's the General?

DIEGO. An altered man. No one's ever seen him so easy. He spends hours each day with the King. He's going to find it hard when he has to do it.

DE SOTO. Do what?

DIEGO. Kill him, sir.

DE SOTO. He can't do that, not after a contract witnessed before a whole army.

DIEGO. Well, he can't let him go, that's for certain. Never mind, he'll find a way. He's as cunning as the devil's grand-dad, saving your pardon, sir.

DE SOTO. No, you're right, boy. He will. He must.'

DIEGO. Tell us about this capital, then. What's it like?

(*The line of* INDIANS, *by this time loaded with the torn-off petals, file slowly round the stage as De Soto describes Cuzco and exit, staggering under the weight of the great gold slabs*)

DE SOTO. Cuzco? It's completely round. They call it the navel of the earth and that's what it looks like. In the middle was a huge temple, the centre of their faith. The walls were plated with gold, enough to blind us. Inside, set out on tables, were golden platters for the sun to dine off.

(*As* DE SOTO *continues, the marvellous objects he tells of appear in the treasure chamber above, borne by* INDIANS, *and are stacked up until they fill it completely. Eventually the interior of the sun is a solid mass of gold*)

Outside, the garden: acres of gold soil planted with gold maize. Entire apple trees in gold. Gold birds on the branches. Gold geese and ducks. Gold butterflies swaying in the air on silver strings. And—imagine this—away in a field, life-size, twenty golden llamas grazing with their kids. The garden of the Sun at Cuzco. A wonder of the earth! Look at it now.   **Light**

DIEGO. Hey, boys! The room's full!   **cue 40**

DOMINGO. It isn't!

SALINAS. It is. Look!

JUAN. He's right. It's full!

DIEGO. We can start the share-out now. (*He cheers*)

PEDRO. What'll you do with your lot, Juan, boy?

JUAN. Buy a farm.

PEDRO. Me, too. I don't work for nobody ever again.

DOMINGO. Ah, you can buy a palace, easy, with a share of that. Never mind a pissing farm! What d'you say, Diego?

DIEGO. Oh, I want a farm. A good stud farm and a stable of Arabs, just for me to ride. What will you have, Salinas?

SALINAS. Me? A bash-house!

(*There is general laughter*)

Open six to six—right in the middle of Trujillo!

(Vasca *enters rolling a huge gold sun, like a hoop*)

Vasca. Look what I got, boys! The sun! He ain't public any more, the old sun. He's private property!

Domingo. There's no private property, till share-out.

Vasca. Well, here's the exception. I risked my life to get this a hundred feet up.

Juan. Dungballs!

Vasca. I did! Off the temple roof.

Pedro. Come on, boys, get it up there with the rest.

Vasca. No. Finding's keeping. That's the law.

Juan. What law?

Vasca. My law. Do you think you'll see any of this once the share-out starts? Not on your pissing life. You leave it up there, boy, you won't see nothing again.

Pedro (*to his brother*) He's right there.

Juan. Do you think so?

Vasca. Of course. Officers first, then the Church. You'll get pissing nothing.

Salinas (*after a pause*) So let's have a share-out now, then!

Domingo. Why not? We're all entitled.

Vasca. Of course you are.

Juan. All right, I'm with you.

Pedro. Good boy!

Salinas. Come on, then.

(*They* All *make a rush for the sun chamber*)

De Soto. Where do you think you're going? You know the orders. Nothing till share-out. Penalty for breach, death. Disperse now. I'll go and see the General.

(*The* Soldiers *hesitate*)

(*Quietly*) Get to your posts.

(*Reluctantly, the* Soldiers *disperse and exit, leaving the sun on the stage.* Diego *follows last*)

And keep a sharp watch. The danger's not over yet.

Diego. I'd say it's only just begun, sir.   **Light cue 41**

(Diego *exits.* De Soto *remains alone.*

Pizarro and Atahuallpa *enter, duelling furiously.*   **Scene vii** Young Martin *follows.* Atahuallpa *is a magnificent fighter and launches himself vigorously on the old man, finally knocking the sword from his hand*)

Pizarro. Enough! You exhaust me . . .

Atahuallpa. I fight well—'ye-es'? (*From the difficulty he has with the word, it is evident that it is in Spanish*)

Pizarro (*imitating him*) 'Ye-es'! Like a hidalgo.
Young Martin. Magnificent, my lord.
Pizarro. I'm proud of you.
Atahuallpa (*clasping his hands*) Chica!
Young Martin (*to Pizarro*) Maize wine, sir.

(*Two* Indians *enter, with wine bowls*)

Pizarro. De Soto! My dear Second . . . (*He drinks*)
De Soto. General!
Pizarro. A drink!
De Soto (*taking a bowl*) With pleasure, sir. (*He drinks*) General,
the room is full.
Pizarro (*casually*) I know it.
De Soto. My advice to you is to share out immediately. The men
are just on the turn.
Pizarro. I think so too.
De Soto. We daren't delay.
Pizarro. Agreed. Now I shall astound you, Cavalier. Atahuallpa,
you have learnt how a Spaniard fights. Now you will learn his
honour. Martin, your pen.

(Young Martin *produces a quill pen and a scroll*)

(*Dictating*) 'Let this be known throughout my army. The Inca
Atahuallpa has today discharged his obligation to General Pizarro.
He is therefore a free man.'
De Soto (*toasting Atahuallpa*) My lord, your freedom!

(Atahuallpa *kneels. Silently he mouths words of gratitude to the Sun*)

Atahuallpa. Atahuallpa thanks the lord De Soto, the lord
Pizarro, all lords of honour. You may touch my joy. (*He extends his
arm*)

(Pizarro *and* De Soto *help to raise Atahuallpa*)

De Soto. What happens now?

(*The* Indians *exit with the bowls*)

Pizarro. I release him. He must swear first, of course, not to harm
us.
De Soto. Do you think he will?
Pizarro. For me he will. For me he will!
Atahuallpa (*to Young Martin*) What is that you have done?
Young Martin. Writing, my lord.
Atahuallpa. Explain this.
Young Martin. These are signs. This is 'Atahuallpa', and this is
'ransom'.
Atahuallpa. You put this sign, and he will see and know 'ran-
som'?

YOUNG MARTIN. Yes.

ATAHUALLPA. No.

YOUNG MARTIN. Yes, my lord. Here, I'll do it again.

ATAHUALLPA. Here, on my nail. Do not say what you put.

(YOUNG MARTIN *writes on Atahuallpa's nail*)

YOUNG MARTIN. Now show it to the Cavalier.

(ATAHUALLPA *shows De Soto the writing.* DE SOTO *reads and whispers the word to Atahuallpa*)

ATAHUALLPA (*to Young Martin*) What is put?

YOUNG MARTIN. God.

ATAHUALLPA (*amazed*) God . . . ! (*He stares at his nail in fascination, then bursts into delighted laughter, like a child*) Show me again! Another sign.

(YOUNG MARTIN *writes on another nail*)

PIZARRO. De Soto!

DE SOTO. Sir!

PIZARRO. Tell Salinas to take five hundred Indians and melt everything down.

DE SOTO. Everything?

PIZARRO. Well, we can't transport it as it is.

DE SOTO. But there are objects of great beauty, sir. In all my service I have never seen treasure like this. Work subtler than anything in Italy. *You can't destroy it all!*

PIZARRO. You're a tender man, Cavalier.

ATAHUALLPA (*extending his nail to Pizarro*) What is put?

PIZARRO (*who, of course, cannot read*) Put?

ATAHUALLPA. Here.

PIZARRO. This is a foolish game.

YOUNG MARTIN. The General never learnt the skill, my lord. (*After an embarrassed pause*) A soldier does not need it.

(ATAHUALLPA *stares at Young Martin*)

ATAHUALLPA. A king needs it. There is great power in these marks. You are the King in this room. You must teach us two. We will learn together—like brothers.

PIZARRO (*eagerly*) You would stay with me here, to learn?

ATAHUALLPA. No. Tomorrow I must go.

PIZARRO. And then? What will you do?

ATAHUALLPA. I will not hurt you.

PIZARRO. Or my army?

ATAHUALLPA. That I not swear.

PIZARRO. But you must.

ATAHUALLPA. You do not say this till now.

PIZARRO. Well, now I say it. Atahuallpa, you must swear to me that you will not harm a man in my army if I let you go.

ATAHUALLPA. This I will not swear.

PIZARRO. For my sake . . . !

ATAHUALLPA. Three thousand of my people they killed in the square. Three thousand, without arms. I will avenge them.

PIZARRO. There is a way of mercy, Atahuallpa.

ATAHUALLPA. It is not my way. It is not your way.

PIZARRO. Well, show it to me, then.

ATAHUALLPA. Keep your swear first.

PIZARRO. That I cannot do.

ATAHUALLPA. Cannot?

PIZARRO. Not immediately—you must see: you are many, we are few.

ATAHUALLPA. This is not important.

PIZARRO. To me it is.

(ATAHUALLPA *hisses with fury. He strides slowly across and Pizarro's face makes a violent gesture with his hand between their two mouths*)

ATAHUALLPA (*violently*) You gave a word!

PIZARRO. And will keep it. Only not now. Not today.

ATAHUALLPA. When?

PIZARRO. Soon.

ATAHUALLPA. When?

PIZARRO. Very soon.

ATAHUALLPA (*falling on his knees and beating the ground*) When?

PIZARRO. As soon as you promise not to harm my army.

ATAHUALLPA (*with wild rage*) I will kill every man of them! I will make drums of their bodies! I will make flutes of their bones! I will beat music on them at my great feasts!

PIZARRO (*provoked*) Boy—what have I put?

YOUNG MARTIN (*reading*) 'He is therefore a free man.'

PIZARRO. Continue: 'But for the welfare of the country, he will remain for the moment as guest of the army.'

DE SOTO. What does that mean?

ATAHUALLPA. What does he say?

PIZARRO. Don't translate.

DE SOTO. So it's started. My warning was nothing to you.

PIZARRO. Well, gloat, gloat!

DE SOTO. I don't gloat.

ATAHUALLPA. What does he say?

PIZARRO. Nothing.

ATAHUALLPA. There is fear in his face!

PIZARRO. Be *quiet*! (*To De Soto; savagely*) I want all the gold in blocks. Leave nothing unmelted. Attend to it yourself, personally.

(DE SOTO *exits abruptly.* OLD MARTIN *appears in the background.* PIZARRO *is trembling*)

(*To Young Martin*) Boy, come here—come here. Now get out.

YOUNG MARTIN. He trusts you, sir.

PIZARRO. Trust, what's that? Another word. Honour—glory—trust: your word—gods!

YOUNG MARTIN. I can see it, sir. He trusts you.

PIZARRO. I told you: out.

YOUNG MARTIN (*greatly daring*) You can't betray him, sir. You can't

PIZARRO. Damn you—impertinence!

YOUNG MARTIN. I don't care, sir. You just can't . . . ! (*He stops*)

PIZARRO. In all your study of those admirable writers, you never learned the duty a page owes his master. I am sorry you have not better fulfilled your first office. There will be no other.

(YOUNG MARTIN *makes to go out*)

A salute, if you please.

(YOUNG MARTIN *bows*)

Time was when we couldn't stop you.   **Light
                                                     cue 42**

(YOUNG MARTIN *exits.* PIZARRO *stares after him, shaking*)

OLD MARTIN. I went out into the night—the cold high night of the Andes, hung with stars like crystal apples, and sat down and dropped my first tears as a man. My first and last. That was my first and last worship, too. Devotion never came again.

(OLD MARTIN *exits, With a moan,* PIZARRO *collapses on the floor down* R *and lies writhing in pain.* ATAHUALLPA *contemplates his captor with surprised disdain. But slowly, as the old man's agony continues, contempt in* ATAHUALLPA *is replaced by a gentler emotion. Curious, he kneels. Uncertain what to do, he extends his hands, first to the wound, and then to Pizarro's head, which he holds with a kind of remote tenderness*)

PIZARRO. Leave it now. There is no cure or more   **Light
easing for it. Death has entered the house, you see. It's   cue 43**
half down already; like an old barn. What can you know
about that? Youth's in you like a spring of blood, to spurt for ever.
Your skin is singing: 'You will never get old.' But Time is stalking
you, as I did. That brass flesh will cold and smudge. Your eyes will
curdle, those wet living eyes. They'll make a mummy of your body—
I know the custom—and wrap you in robes of vicuna wool, and carry
you through all your Empire down to Cuzco. And then they'll fold
you in two and sit you on a chair in darkness! Atahuallpa, we're
going to die! And the thought of that dark has for years rotted everything for me, all simple joy in light. All through old age, which is so
much longer and more terrible than anything in youth, I've watched
the circles of nature with hatred. The leaves pop out, the leaves fall.

Every year it's piglet time, calving time, time for children in a gush of blood and water. Women dote on this. A birth, any birth, fills them with love. They clap with love, and my soul shrugs. Round and round is all I see: an endless sky of birds, flying and ripping and nursing their young to fly and rip and nurse their young—*for what*? Listen, boy. That prison the Priest calls Sin Original, I know as Time. And seen in time everything is trivial. Pain. Good. God is trivial in that seeing. Trapped in this cage we cry out: 'There's a gaoler; there must be. At the last, last, last of lasts he will let us out. He will! He will! But, oh, my boy, no one will come out for all our crying. Listen. The silence is waiting. Not one sound we make can lift it. The darkness, waiting. Not one deed of ours—mercy or anything, or grace can light it up. All we can do is cheat Nature as we can. Feel less, it'll hurt less. (*He pauses*) I'm going to kill you, Atahuallpa. What does it matter? Words kept, words broken, it all means nothing. Nothing. You go to sleep earlier than me, that's all. Do you see? Look at your eyes, like coals from the sun, glowing for ever in the deep of your skull. My dream . . . Sing me your little song. (*Singing*) O little finch . . .

     (ATAHUALLPA *intones a few lines of the song*)

Nothing. Nothing. (*In sudden anguish, almost hatred*) Oh, lad, what am I going to do with you?

     (*A red light appears up above.* OLD MARTIN *enters the*   **Scene viii**
     Sun Chamber. There is violent music, the sound of destruction)
                                              Effects

OLD MARTIN. Nine forges were kept alight for three   **cue 51**
weeks. The masterwork of centuries was banged down
into fat bars, four hundred and forty pounds each day.   **Light**
The booty exceeded all other known in history: the sack   **cue 44**
of Genoa, Milan or even Rome. Share-out started at   **Effects**
once.   **cue 52**

     (OLD MARTIN *exits. The light fades, and comes up on the*   **Light**
     stage, where the SOLDIERS *assemble*)   **cue 45**

DIEGO. General Francisco Pizarro, fifty-seven thousand, two hundred and twenty gold pesos. Hernando de Soto, seventeen thousand, seven hundred and forty gold pesos. The holy Church, two thousand, two hundred and twenty gold pesos.

     (ESTETE *and* DE CANDIA *enter*)

ESTETE. And a fifth of everything, of course, to the Crown.
PIZARRO. You come in good time, Veedor.
ESTETE. So it seems! (*To De Soto*) Cavalier.
DE SOTO. Veedor.
PIZARRO. Welcome, De Candia.
DE CANDIA. Thank you. (*Indicating the ear-ring*) I see the living's

become soft here already. The men hung with jewels like fops at Court.

PIZARRO. You set the fashion: I only follow.

DE CANDIA. I'm flattered.

PIZARRO. What news of the reinforcements?

DE CANDIA. None.

ESTETE. I sent runners back to the coast. They saw nothing.

PIZARRO. So we're cut off here. How's my garrison?

DE CANDIA. Spanish justice reigns supreme. They hang Indians for everything. How's your royal friend? When do we hang him?

(*There is a pause.* PIZARRO *tears off his ear-ring and flings it to the floor*)

PIZARRO (*quietly*) Finish the share-out.

(PIZARRO *exits violently. The* MEN *stare after him*)

DE SOTO. Go on, Diego. Tell us the rest. (*After a pause*) Go on, man!

DIEGO. The remainder—cavalry, infantry, clerks, farriers, coopers and the like—will divide a total of nine hundred and seventy-one thousand gold pesos!

(*The* SOLDIERS *cheer.* RODAS *enters*)

SALINAS. Well, look. Our little tailor! How are you, friend?

RODAS. Hungry. What do I get?

SALINAS. A kick up the tunnel.

RODAS. Ha, ha. Day of a hundred jokes! I got a right to a share.

DOMINGO. What for? What right?

RODAS. I stayed behind and guarded your pissing rear. That's what for.

DE SOTO. You've no right, Rodas. As far as you cared, we could all rot, remember? Well, now you get nothing—the proper wage for cowardice.

(*There is general agreement. The* MEN *move upstage and settle to a game of dice*)

(*To Estete*) I must wait on the General.

ESTETE. I am sorry to see him still subject to distresses. I had hoped that victory would have brought him calmer temper.

DE CANDIA. It must be his new wealth, Veedor. So much, so sudden, must be a great burden to him.

DE SOTO. The burdens of the General, sir, are care for his men, and for our present situation. Let us try to lighten them for him as we can.

(DE SOTO *exits*)

DE CANDIA. Let us indeed. One throat cut and we're all lightened.

ESTETE. It would much relieve the Crown if you'd cut it.

DE CANDIA. If I . . . ? You mean I'm not Spanish, I don't have to trouble with honour!

ESTETE. You're not a subject. It could be disowned by my King. And you have none.

DE CANDIA. So the Palace of Disinterest has a shithouse after all. Veedor, you're the overseer here, so do your job. Go to the General and tell him the brownie must go. And add this from me: if Spain waits any longer, Venice will act for herself.   Light   cue 46

(DE CANDIA *and* ESTETE *exit*. OLD MARTIN *enters. There is a scene of tension and growing violence. The* SOL-DIERS *dice for gold. A line of masked* INDIANS *carrying instruments for making bird noises and guerros enter above and watch the scene silently. A drum begins to beat. As Old Martin speaks,* PIZARRO *stumbles in, and during the whole ensuing scene limps to and fro across the stage like a caged animal, ignoring everything but his mental pain*)   Scene ix

OLD MARTIN. Morale began to go fast. Day after day we watched his private struggle, and the brownies watched us, waiting one sign from the frozen boy to get up and kill the lot of us.   Effects   cue 53

(OLD MARTIN *exits*. JUAN *throws the dice successfully*)

DIEGO. Two fours!

JUAN. That's mine, boy. (*He grabs a gold bar belonging to Pedro*) That's mine, boy.

RODAS. Come on, fellers, cut me in.

SALINAS. Piss off! You lost your stake yesterday!

VASCA. That's right. No stake, no bloody play.

RODAS. Bloody bastards.

DOMINGO. They say there's an army gathering in the mountains. At least five thousand of them.

VASCA. I heard that, too.

(SALINAS *throws dice. The* INDIANS *sound bird cries*)

SALINAS. That's just stories. Pissing stupid stories. You don't want to listen to 'em. Come on!

RODAS. I'd like to see you when they tie you to the stake.

DOMINGO. They say it's led by the Inca's top general. The brownies are full of his name.

RODAS. Yes, that's right .They say he's a pissing cannibal an' all— I've heard his name, it's Rumi— something—Ruminagui!

(*The* INDIANS *above repeat the name in a low menacing chant:* RU-MIN-A-GUI! *The* SOLDIERS *look fearfully about them. The bird cries sound again*)

SALINAS. Come on, then. Let's play.

VASCA. All right. What stake?

SALINAS. The sun!

VASCA (*reluctantly agreeing*) All right. (*He rolls the dice*) Turn up! Turn up! Turn up!

INDIANS. Ruminagui!

VASCA. King and ten. Beat that!

SALINAS. Holy Mary, Mother of Christ. Bare my soul and bless my dice! (*He throws*) Two kings. I'm sorry, lads, but that's the sun gone.

VASCA. Go on, then. Let's see you pick it up.

(SALINAS *bends and tries to shift the sun.* VASCA *laughs. The bird cries grow louder. The guerros sound*)

RODAS. He can't lift it, but I can't play!

SALINAS. I'll settle for these. (*He picks up three gold bars and walks off with them*)

(RODAS *trips him up.* SALINAS *goes sprawling*)

Christ damn you, Rodas—that's the bloody last I take from you.

(SALINAS *springs at Rodas and clouts him with a gold bar.* RODAS *howls, picks up another bar, and a fight starts between them which soon becomes a violent free-for-all. The* MEN *shout; the birds scream;* PIZARRO *paces to and fro, ignoring everything*)

DOMINGO. Help, General!

(*Finally* DE SOTO *rushes on just in time as* SALINAS *tries to strangle* RODAS. *He is followed by* ESTETE, VALVERDE *and* DE NIZZA, *who attend to the wounded*)

DE SOTO. *Stop this!* Do you want to start it all off?   Effects
cue 54

(*Silence falls. All the* INDIANS *rise, above. Uneasily, the* SOLDIERS *stare up at them*)   Light
cue 47

(*To various Soldiers*) You—night-watch! You, you, go with him. You take the East Gate. The rest to quarters. Move!

(*The* SOLDIERS *exit.* ESTETE, VALVERDE, DE SOTO, DE NIZZA *and* PIZARRO *remain*)

DE SOTO (*to Pizarro*) Mutiny's smoking. Act now or   Scene x
it'll be a blaze you'll not put out.

PIZARRO. What do I do?

DE SOTO. Take our chances, what else can we do? You have to let him go.

PIZARRO. And what happens then? A tiny army is wiped out in five minutes, and the whole story lost for always. Later someone else will conquer Peru and no one will even remember my name.

De Soto. What kind of name will they remember if you kill him?

Pizarro. A conqueror. That at least.

De Soto. A man who butchered his prisoner after giving his word. There's a name for your ballads.

Pizarro. I'll never live to hear them. What do I care? What does it matter? Whatever I do, what does it matter?

De Soto. Nothing, if you don't feel it. But I think you do.

Pizarro. Let me understand you. As Second-in-Command, you counsel certain death for this army?

De Soto. I'll not counsel his.

Pizarro. Then you counsel the death of Christ in this country, as you told my page boy months ago?

De Soto. That's not known.

Pizarro. As good.

De Soto. No. Christ is love. Love is . . .

Pizarro. What? *What?*

De Soto. Now in him. He trusts you, trust him. It's all you can do.

Pizarro. Have you gone soft in the head? What's this chorus now? 'Trust! Trust.' You know the law out here: kill or get killed. You said it yourself. The mercies come later.

De Soto. Not for you. I wish to God you'd never made this bargain. But you did. Now you've no choice left.

Pizarro. No, this is my kingdom. In Peru I am absolute. I have choice always.

De Soto. You had it. But you made it.

Pizarro. Then I'll take it back.

De Soto. Then you never made it. I'm not playing words, General. There's no choice where you don't stick by it.

Pizarro. I can *choose* to take it back.

De Soto. No, sir. That would only be done on orders from your own fear. That's not choosing.

Estete. May the Crown be allowed a word?

Pizarro. I know your word. Death.

Estete. What else can it be?

Valverde. Your army is in terror. Do you care nothing for them?

Pizarro *(to De Soto)* Well, Cavalier. Do you?

De Soto. I care for them. But less than I care for you. God knows why.

(De Soto *exits*)

Estete. The issue is simple. You are Viceroy here, ruling in the name of the King who sent you. You have no right to risk his land for any reason at all.

Pizarro. And tell me what did this King ever do for me? Gave me leave to bring him a fortune, granted me a salary if I found money to pay it. Allowed me governance if I got land to govern. Magnificent: if I'd failed this time he'd have cast me off with one shrug of his royal feathers. Well, now I cast him. Francisco Pizarro casts off Carlos the Fifth. Go and tell them. (*He sits slowly, in the manner of Atahuallpa*)

ESTETE. This is ridiculous.

PIZARRO. No doubt, but you'll have to give me better argument before I give him up.

ESTETE. Perverse man, what is Atahuallpa to you?

PIZARRO. Someone I promised life.

ESTETE. Promised life? How quaint. The sort of chivalry idea you pretend to despise. If you want to be an absolute king, my man, you must learn to act out of personal will. Break your word just *because* you gave it. Till then, you're only a pig-man trying to copy his betters.

(PIZARRO *rounds on Estete angrily*)

VALVERDE. My son, listen to me. No promise to a pagan need bind a Christian. Simply think what's at stake: the lives of a hundred and seventy of the faithful. Are you going to sacrifice them for one savage?

PIZARRO. You know lives have no weight, Father. Ten can't be added up to outbalance one.

VALVERDE. Ten good can against one evil. And this man is evil. His people kiss his hands as the source of life.

PIZARRO. As we do yours. All your days you play at being God. You only hate my Inca because he does it better.

VALVERDE. *What?*

PIZARRO. Dungballs to all churches that are or ever could be! How I hate you. 'Kill who I bid you kill and I will pardon it.' YOU with your milky fingers forcing in the blade. How dare you priests bless any man who goes slicing into battle? But no. You slice with him. 'Rip!' you scream. 'Tear! Blind! In the name of Christ!' Tell me, soft Father, if Christ was here now, do you think he would kill my Inca?

(DIEGO *rushes on*)

DIEGO. Sir! Sir! Another fight broke out, sir. There's one dead.

PIZARRO. Who?

DIEGO. Blas. He drew a knife. I only meant to spit his leg, but he slipped and got it through the guts.

PIZARRO. You did well to punish fighting.

DIEGO. May I speak free, sir?

PIZARRO. What? I've got to kill him, is that it?

DIEGO. What other way is there? The men are out of their wits. They feel death all round them.

PIZARRO. So it is and let them face it. I promised them gold, not life. Well; they've got gold. The cripples have gold crutches. The coughers spit gold snot. The bargain's over.

T036108

DIEGO. No, sir, not for me. To me you're the greatest General in the world. And we're the greatest company.

PIZARRO. Pizarro's boys, is that it?

DIEGO. That's it. Yes, sir. Pizarro's boys.

PIZARRO. Ah, the old band. The dear old regiment. Fool! Look, you were born a man. Not a Blue man, or a Green man, but a MAN. You are able to feel a thousand separate loves unordered by fear or by solitude. Are you going to trade them all in for Gang-love? Flag-love? Carlos-the-Fifth-love? Jesus-the-Christ-love? All that has been tied on you; it is only this that makes you bay for death.

VALVERDE. I'll give you death. When I get back to Spain a commission will hale you to the stake for what you have said today.

PIZARRO. If I let the Inca go, Father, you'll never get back to Spain.

ESTETE. You madman: see here, you put him underground by sunset or I'll take the knife to him myself.

PIZARRO (*to De Nizza*) Well, come on, Brother De Nizza, you're the lord of answers—why so silent? Will you join him—will you take the knife to him as well?

DE NIZZA. Don't try to trap me. I know as well as you how terrible it is to kill. But worse is to spare evil. When I came here first I thought I had found Paradise. Now I know it is Hell. A country which castrates its people. What are your Inca subjects? A population of eunuchs, living entirely without choice.

PIZARRO. And what are your Christians? Unhappy hating men. Look: I am a peasant, I want value for money. If I go marketing for gods, who do I buy? Christ of Europe with all its deaths and brooding, or Atahuallpa of Peru? His spirit keeps an Empire sweet and still as corn in the field.

DE NIZZA. And you're content to be a stalk of corn?

PIZARRO. Yes, yes! They're no fools, these sun men. They know what cheats you sell on your barrow. Choice. Hunger. Tomorrow. Well, they've looked at your wares and passed on. They live here as part of nature, no hope and no despair.

DE NIZZA. And no life. Why must you be so dishonest? You are not only part of nature, and you know it. There is something in you at *war* with nature; there is in all of us. Something that does not belong in you the animal. What do you think it is? What is this pain in you that month after month makes you hurl yourself against the cage of time? This is God, driving you to accept divine eternity. Take it, General: not this pathetic copy of eternity the Incas have tried to make on earth. Peru is a sepulchre of the soul. For the sake of the free spirit in each of us it must be destroyed.

PIZARRO. So, there is Christian charity. To save my own soul I must kill another man!

DE NIZZA. To save love in the world you must kill lovelessness.

PIZARRO. Hail to you, sole judge of love! No salvation outside your church: and no love either. Oh, your arrogance . . . (*Simply*)

I do not know love, Father, but what can I ever know, if I
feel none for him? (*He pauses, then cries out with full power*)   **Effects**
Atahuallpa!   **cue 55**

> (*Music.* ATAHUALLPA *enters, followed by* YOUNG MARTIN. PIZARRO
> *scrambles to his feet*)

They ache for your death! They want to write psalms to their God
in your blood, but they'll all die before you, that I promise! (*He
binds Atahuallpa's arm to his own with a long cord of rope, last used to tie some
gold*) There.

> (ATAHUALLPA *attempts to move away*)

No, no, come here. Now no one will kill you unless they kill me first.
ESTETE. De Candia!

> (DE CANDIA *enters, with a drawn sword*)

DE CANDIA. A touching game—gaolers and prisoners. But it's over
now. General, do you think I'm going to die so that you can dance
with a darkie? (*He draws his sword*)

> (PIZARRO *pulls the sword from* YOUNG MARTIN'S *scabbard*)

DIEGO (*drawing*) Sorry, sir, but it's got to be done.
ESTETE (*drawing*) There's nothing you can do, Pizarro. The whole
camp's against you.
PIZARRO. De Soto!
DE CANDIA. If De Soto raises his sword, he'll lose the arm that
swings it.
PIZARRO. You'll lose yours first. Come on!

> (PIZARRO *rushes at De Candia, but* ATAHUALLPA *gives a growl and
> pulls him back by the rope. There is a pause,* PIZARRO *falls to the floor*)

ATAHUALLPA. You are nothing.
PIZARRO. I command here still. They will obey me.
ATAHUALLPA. They will kill me though you cry curses of earth and
sky. (*To them all*) Leave us. I will speak with him.

> (*Impressed by the command in his voice,* ALL *exit save*   **Light**
> PIZARRO—*now roped to his prisoner—and* YOUNG MARTIN)   **cue 48**

(*Crouching and pulling on the rope*) It is no matter. They
cannot kill me.   **Scene xi**
PIZARRO. Cannot?
ATAHUALLPA. Man who dies cannot kill a God who lives for ever.
PIZARRO. I wouldn't bet on that, my lord.
ATAHUALLPA. Only my father can take me from here. And he
would not accept me killed by men like you. Men with no word. You
may be King of this land, but never God. I am God of the Four
Quarters, and if you kill me tonight I will rise at dawn when *my*

Father first touches *my* body with light.

PIZARRO. Do you believe this?

ATAHUALLPA. All my people know it—it is why they have let me stay with you.

PIZARRO. They knew you could not be harmed . . .

ATAHUALLPA. So.

PIZARRO. Was this the meaning? The meaning of my dream? You were choosing me?

YOUNG MARTIN. My lord, it's just a boast. Beyond any kind of reason.

PIZARRO. Is it?

YOUNG MARTIN. How can a man die, then get up and walk away?

PIZARRO. Let's hear your creed, boy. 'I believe in Jesus Christ, the Son of God, that he suffered under Pontius Pilate, was crucified, dead and buried . . . ' and what?

YOUNG MARTIN. Sir?

PIZARRO. What?

YOUNG MARTIN. 'He descended into hell, and on the third day he rose again from the dead . . .' (*His voice gives out*)

PIZARRO. You don't believe it!

YOUNG MARTIN. I do! On my soul! I believe with perfect faith!

PIZARRO. But Christ's is to be the only one, is that it? What if it was possible—here in a land beyond all maps and scholars—guarded by mountains up to the sky, that there were true gods on earth, creators of true peace? Think of it! Gods, free of time!

YOUNG MARTIN. It's impossible my lord.

PIZARRO. It's the only way to give life meaning! To blast out, unshackle time and live for ever, us in our own persons. This is the law, Martin; die in despair or be a god yourself! Look at him: always so calm as if the teeth of life never bit him—or the teeth of death. What if it were really true, Martin? That I've gone God-hunting and caught one. A being who can renew his life over and over?

YOUNG MARTIN. But how can that be, sir? How could any man?

PIZARRO. By returning over and over again to the source of life— *to the Sun!*

YOUNG MARTIN. No, sir . . .

PIZARRO. Why not? What else is a god but what we know we can't do without? The flowers that worship it, the sunflowers in their soil, are us after night, after cold and lightless days, turning our faces towards it, adoring. The sun is the only god I know! We eat you to walk. We drink you to sing. Our reins loosen under you and we laugh. Even I laugh, here! I laugh! (*He recalls his attempt to dancing*)

YOUNG MARTIN. General, you need rest, sir.

PIZARRO (*after a pause*) Yes. Yes—yes. (*Bitterly*) How clever. He's understood every word I've said to him these awful months— all my secret pain he's heard, and this is his revenge. This silly joke. How he must hate me. (*Tightening the rope*) Oh yes, you cunning bastard. Look, Martin—behold my god. I have the Sun on a string!

I can make it rise—(*He pulls Atahuallpa's arm up*)—or set! (*He throws Atahuallpa to his knees down* R)

YOUNG MARTIN. General . . .!

PIZARRO. I'll make you set for ever! Two can joke as well as one. You want your freedom? All right, you're free! Go on. (*He starts circling round Atahuallpa*) Walk out of the camp! They may stop you, but what's that to you? You're invulnerable. They may knock you down, but your father the Sun will pick you up again. Go on! Get up! . . . Go on! . . . Get up! Go on! . . . Go on! . . . Go on! . . . Go on! . . . Go on! . . . Go on! (*He breaks into a frantic gallop round and round Atahuallpa, the rope at full stretch*)

(ATAHUALLPA *turns with him, somersaulting then holding him, his teeth bared with the strain, as if breaking a wild horse, until* PIZARRO *tumbles exhausted to the ground. Silence follows, broken only by deep moaning from the stricken man. Quietly* ATAHUALLPA *pulls in the rope. Then at last he speaks*)

ATAHUALLPA. Pizarro. You will die soon and you do not believe in your God. It is why you tremble and keep no word. Believe in me. I will bring you a word and fill you with joy. For you I will do a great thing. I will swallow death and spit it out of me.

(*There is a pause. The whole scene stays very still*)

PIZARRO. No, no. You cannot.

ATAHUALLPA. Yes, if my father will sit.

PIZARRO. What if he does not?

ATAHUALLPA. He will. His people still need me. Believe.

PIZARRO. No, it's impossible.

ATAHUALLPA. Believe.

PIZARRO. How? How? How?

ATAHUALLPA. You must accept my priest power.

PIZARRO (*quietly*) Oh, no! You go or not as you choose, but I take nothing more in this world.   **Light**
cue 49

ATAHUALLPA. Take my word. Take my peace. I will put water to your wound, old man. Believe . . .

(*There is a long silence. The* LIGHTS *are now fading around him*)

PIZARRO. What must I do?

(OLD MARTIN *enters.* ATAHUALLPA *mimes the rite which Old Martin describes*)

OLD MARTIN. How can I speak now and hope to be believed? As night fell like a hand over the eye, and great white stars sprang out over the snow-rim of our world, Atahuallpa confessed Pizarro. He did it in the Inca manner. He took Ichu grass and a stone. Into the Ichu grass the General spoke for an hour or more. None heard what he said save the King, who could not understand it. Then the King struck him on the back with the stone, cast away the grass, and made the signs for purification.

PIZARRO. If any blessing is in me, take it and go. Fly up, my bird, and come to me again.

(ATAHUALLPA *takes a knife from* YOUNG MARTIN *and cuts the rope. Then he walks upstage. All the* OFFICERS *and* MEN *enter. During the following a pole is set up above, in the sun, and* ATAHUALLPA *is hauled up into it*)

Light cue 50

OLD MARTIN. The Inca was tried by a court quickly mustered. He was accused of usurping the throne and killing his brother; of idolatry and of having more than one wife. On all these charges he was found . . .

Scene xii

Effects cue 56

VALVERDE. Guilty.
ESTETE. Guilty.
DE CANDIA. Guilty.

Effects cue 57

OLD MARTIN. Sentence to be carried out the same night.

ESTETE. Death by burning.

Light cue 51

(*The* LIGHTS *come up in the sun.* ATAHUALLPA *gives a great cry*)

PIZARRO. No! He must not burn! His body must stay in one piece!

VALVERDE. Let him repent his idolatry and be baptized a Christian. He will receive the customary mercy.

OLD MARTIN. Strangling instead.

PIZARRO. You must do it! Deny your father! If you don't you will be burnt to ashes. There will be no flesh left for him to warm alive at dawn.

(YOUNG MARTIN *screams and runs from the stage in horror*)

You must do it.

(*In a gesture of surrender,* ATAHUALLPA *kneels*)

OLD MARTIN. So it was that Atahuallpa came to Christ.

(DE NIZZA *enters above, with a bowl of water*)

DE NIZZA. I baptize you Juan de Atahuallpa, in honour of Juan the Baptist, whose sacred day this is.

ESTETE. The twenty-ninth of August, fifteen hundred and thirty-three.

VALVERDE. And may our Lord and his angels receive your soul with joy?

SOLDIERS. Amen!

(ATAHUALLPA *suddenly raises his head, tears off his clothes and intones in a great voice*)

ATAHUALLPA. INTI! INTI! INTI!   **Effects**
VALVERDE. What does he say?   **cue 58**
PIZARRO (*intoning also*) The Sun. The Sun. The Sun.   **Light**
VALVERDE. *Kill him!*   **cue 52**

(SOLDIERS *haul Atahuallpa to his feet and hold him to the
stake.* RODAS *slips a string over his head. There is a low light drumming.
While all the* SPANIARDS *below recite the Latin creed and great howls of
'Inca!' come from the darkness, the Sovereign King of Peru
is garrotted. His screams and struggles subside; his body falls*   **Effects**
slack. His executioners hand the body down to the SOLDIERS   **cue 59**
*below, who carry it to the centre of the stage and drop it at
Pizarro's feet. Then* ALL *exit except* PIZARRO, *who stands as if turned
to stone.*

A drum beats. Slowly, in semi-darkness, the stage fills with INDIANS,
*robed in black and terracotta, wearing the great golden funeral masks
of ancient Peru. Grouped round the prone body, they intone a
strange chant of resurrection, punctuated by hollow beats on*   **Light**
the drum and by long, long silences in which they turn their   **cue 53**
immense triangular eyes inquiringly up to the sky)

INCA LAMENT

INCA	ENGLISH TRANSLATION
Inca yayallay Janaj pachapi	O Inca my father now in heaven
Numa Illakilla Ritinki ari	Thou seest me how I am unfortunate
Kayta Jusapa Massa wommni	and wretched. Yet I do not die
Shungo Tliyispa Kausarishuani	In spite of all, I do not die, my heart is torn from my bosom, yet I live on
Sapa Inca	Unique God
Huaccha Cuyac	friend of the humble
Quya	Queen
Pachacutic ⎫ Viracocha ⎭	Gods
Inti Cori	Son of the Sun

(*Finally, after three great cries of* 'Inca'! *appear to summon it, the
sun rises. Its rays fall on the body.* ATAHUALLPA *does not move. The
masked men watch in amazement—disbelief—finally, despair. Slowly,
with hanging, dejected heads, they shuffle away.* PIZARRO *is*   **Effects**
left alone with the dead King. He contemplates him. A   **cue 60**
*silence. Then suddenly he slaps it viciously, and the body rolls
over on its back*)

PIZARRO. Cheat! You've cheated me! Cheat . . . (*For a
moment his old body is racked with sobs; then, surprised, he feels tears on his*

cheek, He examines them.) What's this? What is it? In all your life you never made one of these, I know, and I not till this minute. Look. (*He kneels to show the dead Inca*) Ah, no. You have no eyes for me now, Atahuallpa. They are dusty balls of amber I can tap on. You have no peace for me, Atahuallpa: the birds still scream in your forest. You have no joy for me, Atahuallpa, my boy: the only joy is in death. I lived between two hates: I die between two darks: blind eyes and blind sky. And yet you saw once. The sky sees nothing, but you saw. Is their comfort there? The sky knows no feeling, but we know them that's sure. Martin's hope, and de Soto's honour, and your trust—your trust which hunted me: we alone make these. That's some marvel, yes, some marvel. To sit in an old cold silence, and sing out sweet with just our own warm breath: that's some marvel, surely. To make water in a sand world: surely, surely . . . God's just a name on your nail; and naming begins cries and cruelties. But to live without hope of after, and make whatever God there is, oh, that's some immortal business surely. I'm tired. Where are you? You're so cold. I'd warm you if I could. But there's no warming now, not ever now. I'm colding, too. There's a snow of death falling all round us. You can almost see it. It's over, lad. I'm coming after you. There's nothing but peace to come. We'll be put into the same earth, father and son in our own land. And that sun will roam uncaught over his empty pasture.

(OLD MARTIN *enters*)

OLD MARTIN. So fell Peru. We gave her greed, hunger and the Cross: three gifts for the civilized life. The family groups that sang on the terraces are gone. In their place slaves shuffle underground and they don't sing there. Peru is a silent country, frozen in avarice. So fell Spain, gorged with gold; distended; now dying.

PIZARRO (*singing*) See that black bird, nailed on a branch,

O little finch . . .!

OLD MARTIN. And so fell you, General my master, whom men called the Son of His Own Deeds. He was killed later in a quarrel with his partner who brought up the reinforcements. But to speak truth, he sat down that morning and never really got up again.

PIZARRO (*singing*) She is cut up, O little finch . . .!

OLD MARTIN. I'm the only one left now of the company: land-owner—slave driver—and forty years from any time of hope. It put out a good blossom, but it was shaken off rough. After that I reckon the fruit always comes sour and doesn't sweeten up much with age.

PIZARRO (*singing*) For stealing grain, O little finch . . .

OLD MARTIN. General, you did for me, and now I've done for you. And there's no joy in that. Or in anything now. But then there's no joy in the world could match me for what I had when I first went with you across the water to find the gold country. And no pain like losing it. Save you all. **Light cue 54**

(OLD MARTIN *goes out.* PIZARRO *lies beside the body of Atahuallpa and quietly sings to it*)

PIZARRO (*singing*) See, see the fate, O little finch,
  Of robber birds, O little finch.

(*The sun glares at the audience*)

FURNITURE AND PROPERTY LIST

ACT I

On stage: Large metal medallion, quartered by four black crucifixes sharpened to resemble swords (on back wall)

Off stage: Wooden stick (YOUNG MARTIN)
Roll of cloth (DE SOTO)
Banners (VILLAGERS)
Large wooden Christ (VALVERDE)
Arquebus (DE CANDIA)
Drum (YOUNG MARTIN)
Pole with image of the sun (MANCO)
Llama head (VILLAC UMU)
Bible (VALVERDE)
Large bloodstained cloth (INDIANS)
Halberds (SPANIARDS)

ACT II

Off stage: Pack of cards (YOUNG MARTIN)
Small cymbals and bells (INDIANS)
Cloak, for Atahuallpa (INDIANS)
Turquoise collar, for Atahuallpa (INDIANS)
Ear-rings, for Atahuallpa (INDIANS)
Musical dishes (INDIANS)
Bowl of meat (OELLO)
Gold utensils and ornaments, plates, apple trees, birds, geese, ducks, butterflies, llamas, etc. (INDIANS)
Dagger (YOUNG MARTIN)
Large gold sun (VASCA)
2 wine bowls (INDIANS)
Quill pen (YOUNG MARTIN)
Scroll (YOUNG MARTIN)
Dice (SPANIARDS)
Guerros and bird-call instruments (INDIANS)
Knife (YOUNG MARTIN)
Pole (SPANIARDS)
Bowl of water (DE NIZZA)
Length of string (RODAS)

LIGHTING PLOT

Property fittings required: nil.
A bare stage, with upper chamber up C. The same scene throughout.
THE MAIN ACTING AREAS extend over the whole stage.

ACT I

Cue 19	OLD MARTIN: '. . . ringing the Valley.'	(Page 21)
	Check to night lighting	
Cue 20	DIEGO: '. . . and I mean that.'	(Page 23)
	Fade to down R *and* C	
Cue 21	PIZARRO: 'I feel just this . . .'	(Page 25)
	Build to general warm lighting	
Cue 22	OLD MARTIN: 'Ten hours passed.'	(Page 26)
	Slow fade to night	
Cue 23	PIZARRO: '. . . gods with weapons.'	(Page 28)
	Fade to downstage lighting	
Cue 24	PIZARRO: 'Now! Now! Now!'	(Page 28)
	Slow build to general warm lighting	
Cue 25	VALVERDE: 'San Jago!'	(Page 29)
	Bring up Sun	
Cue 26	At end of MASSACRE	(Page 30)
	Fade to Black-out	

ACT II

To open:	Black-out	
Cue 27	As LAMENT is intoned	(Page 31)
	Bring up general lighting to ¼	
Cue 28	YOUNG MARTIN enters	(Page 31)
	Build up general stage lighting	
Cue 29	PIZARRO: 'Let's meet this King.'	(Page 32)
	Cross-fade stage lighting down, Sun up	
Cue 30	PIZARRO exits	(Page 33)
	Further fade of stage lighting	
Cue 31	ATAHUALLPA: '. . . my people will suffer.'	(Page 34)
	Build stage lighting, fade Sun	
Cue 32	OLD MARTIN: '. . . nine feet high.'	(Page 35)
	Build Sun, and glow on stage	
Cue 33	ATAHUALLPA: '. . . prison of clouds!'	(Page 36)
	Take out Sun	
Cue 34	OLD MARTIN: '. . . more comfortable state.'	(Page 36)
	Build to 'dressing scene'	
Cue 35	OLD MARTIN: '. . . with sweet potatoes.'	(Page 36)
	Build down R *and upstage*	
Cue 36	DE NIZZA: '. . . help me from it'	(Page 39)
	Build up C *and Sun, fade rest of stage*	
Cue 37	OLD MARTIN: '. . . satisfied with that.'	(Page 39)
	Build stage, fade Sun	
Cue 38	PIZARRO: 'You make me laugh.'	(Page 43)
	Build Sun	
Cue 39	DIEGO: 'Welcome back, sir.'	(Page 43)
	Slight build up C, *take out Sun surround*	
Cue 40	DE SOTO: 'Look at it now!'	(Page 44)
	Build general stage lighting	

Cue 41	DIEGO: '. . . only just begun, sir.' *Stage lighting up full, Sun out*	(Page 45)
Cue 42	PIZARRO: '. . . couldn't stop you.' *Start closing lighting to down* R	(Page 49)
Cue 43	PIZARRO: 'Leave it now.' *Fade lighting except down* R	(Page 49)
Cue 44	PIZARRO: '. . . to do with you?' *Bring up Sun, and general glow on stage*	(Page 50)
Cue 45	OLD MARTIN: '. . . started at once.' *Bring up stage to full, take out Sun*	(Page 50)
Cue 46	DE CANDIA: '. . . act for herself.' *Fade to night lighting, build up Indians above*	(Page 52)
Cue 47	DE SOTO: '. . . start it all off?' *Build stage lighting to full*	(Page 53)
Cue 48	General exit *Fade upstage lighting*	(Page 57)
Cue 49	PIZARRO: '. . . in this world.' *Fade lighting except down* R	(Page 59)
Cue 50	General entrance *Fade stage lighting, build up Sun*	(Page 60)
Cue 51	OLD MARTIN: '. . . the same night.' *Bring up Sun to full*	(Page 60)
Cue 52	PIZARRO: 'The Sun.' *Fade Sun out. Red light on stage*	(Page 61)
Cue 53	Inca LAMENT starts *Take out stage lighting, bring in Sun beams*	(Page 61)
Cue 54	OLD MARTIN: 'Save you all.' *Fade to Black-out*	(Page 62)

EFFECTS

ACT I

Sound Cue No.	Word or Action Cue	Tapes	Score	Vocal Score
1	I have to root for mine like the pigs. It's amusing.	Organ Starts A		
2	*Old Martin Comes In*	Fade Down Organ Slightly A		
3	*Enter Estete*	Fade Up Organ Slightly A		
4	Take the banners out . . .	Fade Organ Up More A		
5	*The boy is frightened and concerned*	Fade Down Organ A		
6	What is it, sir?	Fade Out Organ A		
7	Not by me. By the forest.		The Opening of The Sun 1	The Opening of The Sun
8	all must see him.		End of Court Scene 2	
9	As Scene Four Commences	Burst of Bird Song A	End of Score Cue 2	
10	Take that, Anti Christ.		Atahuallpa Warned 3	
11	If he is no God—he will die!	Short Burst of Bird Cries A	End of Score Cue 3	
		Fade Up Bird Cries B & C		
12	get the blacksmith to cut us out.	Short Burst of Bird Cries A		
13	I'll cut you out.	Short Burst of Bird Cries A		
14	She can stop a horse at five hundred paces.	Short Burst of Bird Cries A		

15	which otherwise it would never feel	Short Burst of Bird Cries	A
16	to think of yourselves as the thieves you are.	Short Burst of Bird Cries	A
17	this is the first who makes me afraid.	Short Burst of Bird Cries	A
18	you'll see a kind of death.	Short Burst of Bird Cries	A
19	Listen, Martin,	Short Burst of Bird Cries	A
20	listen to them.	Fade Out Slowly	B & C
21	the beak to do it.	Short Burst of Bird Cries	A
22	blot up the blood.	Short Burst of Bird Cries	A
23	to feed cats.	Short Burst of Bird Cries	A
24	I'll hurt you past believing.	Short Burst of Bird Cries	A
25	Have the sentries changed?	Short Burst of Bird Cries	A
26	between two hates?	Short Burst of Bird Cries	A
		Fade Up Bird Cries	B & C
27	How is your wound tonight?	Short Burst of Bird Cries	A
28	Then show it to the birds.	Short Burst of Bird Cries	A

Sound Cue No.	Word or Action Cue	Tape A	Score	Vocal Score
29	As Scene Six Commences	Fade Down Bird Cries A Fade Down Bird Cries B & C		
30	witness of a great empire.	Fade Out Bird Cries A Fade Out Bird Cries B & C	Introduction to Toil Song 4	The Toil Song
31	He sees you now.		Embassy Music 5	
32	What I say, I do.		Embassy Exit 6	
33	A god and all his priests. Praise Father Sun!		The Chants of Praise 7	Indian Chants of Praise
34	and stay with you all. Amen.	Te Deum Starts	Ascent of the Andes 8	
35	PIZARRO. Perfect.	Te Deum Fades Out		
36	the Virgin of the Conception, and I mean that.			
37	All remain absolutely still.		The Procession into the Massacre 9a. Bells only until	
38	You don't approach Gods with weapons. Now, Now, Now!		The Procession into the Massacre 9a	
39			The Procession into the Massacre 9b	
40	Silence Falls. The King glares about him.		End of Score Cue 9b	
41	San Jago!		The Massacre 10	
ACT II				
42	Before Act Two commences			1st Inca Lament
43	De Soto Enters			End of Inca Lament

No.	Cue		
44	The mark on the wall was nine feet high.	The Command for Gold 11 End of Score Cue 11	
45	free your Sun from his prison of clouds.		
46	He claps his hands, once.	The Clothing of Atahuallpa 12 End of Score Cue 12 1st Gold Procession 13	The Clothing of Atahuallpa
47	Felipillo knocks it from her hand.		
48	You know this, too, so help me from it.		
49	Their God is not in your face.	2nd Gold Procession 14	Little Finch Song
50	Before Scene Six Commences and during beginning of Scene		
51	As Scene Eight Commences	The Melting of the Gold 15 End of Score Cue 15 The Dice Scene 16 End of Score Cue 16 Atahuallpa Called 17. End when A reaches P	
52	Share-out started at once.		
53	Morale began to go fast.		
54	Stop this!		
55	PIZARRO. Atahuallpa!		
56	The Inca was tried by a court quickly mustered.	The Garrotting of Atahuallpa 18a End of Score Cue 18a The Garrotting 18b	
57	Guilty, Guilty, Guilty. INTI. INTI. INTI.		
58 continuous with 59	Atahuallpa Screams		
60	Pizarro is left alone with the dead King.	Final Lament End of Final Lament	Final Lament End of Final Lament

In the London Production three tapes were used. Tapes B and C were fed to differently placed speakers, but were always used together. They can be supplied separately or merged.

SCHEDULE OF MUSIC

LIST OF MUSIC IN SCORE

1. Recorded Organ Music (4 min. 45 sec.)
2. Opening of the Sun (35–40 sec.)—orchestra and chants
3. End of the Court scene (15–45 sec.)—orchestral
4. Atahuallpa's invitation to Pizarro—orchestral
5. The bird cries in the forest (up to 6 min.)—4 tracks of recorded bird cries plus Indians on 'bird flutes' and guerros
6. Introduction to 'Toil Song'—orchestral
7. 'Toil Song'—Indian singing with small marracas and small drum
8. Villac Umu's Embassy: arrival (5 sec.) exit (5 sec.) orchestral
9. Indian Chants of Praise—orchestra and chants
10. Offstage Spanish Te Deum—recorded Spanish chanting
11. Climbing of the Andes (up to 6 min.)—orchestral (2 flexatons)
12. Procession into Cajamarca (1 min.–1 min. 20 sec.)—orchestra, plus Indians playing bells, cymbals, 'thumb pianos', marracas (large)
13. The Massacre (1 min.–1 min. 30 sec.)—orchestra plus bells on Indians
14. 1st Indian Lament—chant
15. Atahuallpa's Command for Gold (35 sec.)—orchestral
16. Clothing of Atahuallpa and his meal—Indians hum and play crotales, 'musical plates' and 'thumb pianos'
17. 1st Gold Procession—orchestra plus Indian humming
18. 'Little Finch' song—Atahuallpa sings
19. 2nd Gold Procession—orchestra plus Indian humming
20. The Dice Scene—orchestra plus Indian menaces; Indians play bird flutes and guerros
21. The Garotting of Atahuallpa—orchestra
22. Indian Chants of Resurrection—orchestra and chants

INSTRUMENTATION OF SCORE
(Orchestra: four percussionists)

Indians play the following on stage
- 2 drums (Indian 'tablas' or 2 pairs of bongos)
- 2 suspended cymbals on 'Indian handles'
- 2 pairs very large marracas
- 1 pair very small marracas on long handles
- 4 guerros
- 2 dozen bamboo 'bird flutes' (slide recorders) (these can be obtained from any shop specializing in folk craft from India)
- 2 'thumb pianos' (cigar box type sounding board with spring steel tongues which should be hit with light, hard sticks)

Orchestral instruments, divided between four percussion players
   6 suspended cymbals
   4 pairs of bongos
   1 big drum
   1 xylophone
   1 glockenspiel
   2 lion roar drums (string drums)
   2 guerros
   5 triangles
   3 pairs crotales (small cymbals)
   2 sets of sleigh bells
   1 woodblock
   4 slapsticks
   1 large flexaton (musical saw; blade approximately 5 ft. 6 in. long)
   1 small flexaton

THE MASSACRE

All Indians have small bells sewn along their sleeves in the Massacre (and the Procession into Cajamarca). Insofar as their movements are rhythmed, and in time with the orchestral music, this helps to keep the centre of musical (as well as dramatic) attention on stage. There is a section in the orchestral score of the Massacre which is almost completely silent, to enhance this effect.

THE BIRD CRIES IN THE FOREST (1ST ACT)

THE DICE SCENE (*Ruminagui*) (2ND ACT)

In both these scenes the Indians play loud interjections to word cues on both 'bird flutes' and guerros, as a counterpart either to the recording of bird cries, or the orchestral music, to bring closer the sense of threat and danger to the centre of dramatic attention.

TOIL SONG

As the Indians come on the stage they all hum this tune, accompanied by the two women, one woman playing small marracas (one marraca to each beat), the other beating the exact rhythm on a small drum (perhaps a 'tabla' wood drum). When work commences the two women sing the song twice, then all resume humming as the Spaniards speak until all workers are off stage.

LITTLE FINCH

This should be sung very simply with no 'rubato'. Accentuation and dynamics must depend on the meaning of the words. The glissandi should be as the swooping of a bird of prey.

THE HUMMINGS

Atahuallpa's Dressing Scene and meal:

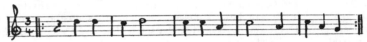

All Indians should hum this tune throughout the scene.

The Indians who help to dress Atahuallpa all have one pair of suspended crotales (ancient Chinese cymbals) hanging from each wrist (about 15 inches of string to each crotale). The Indians who bring on food and feed Atahuallpa have no crotales, but the gold plates should have many small bells hanging below the rims. The plates should also have double bottoms (the lower ones are drum skins). Dried peas or gravel should be inserted between the two bottoms, thus turning the plates into rattles. These plates should be 'played' as they are carried onstage and until Atahuallpa receives his first morsel of food. During Atahuallpa's meal, plates and crotales are silent, the humming continues accompanied by two 'thumb pianos' (pitch ad libitum, to the rhythm of the 'Toil Song')

THE GOLD PROCESSIONS

Hum the TOIL SONG at a lower pitch, *slow*.

Learning
Resource Centre
Stockton
Riverside College

MADE AND PRINTED IN GREAT BRITAIN BY
LATIMER TREND & COMPANY LTD PLYMOUTH
MADE IN ENGLAND